When Knowledge Sparks a Flame

Christina Lechner-Kreidl/Werner Hilweg
Mai Nguyen-Feichtner/Rüdiger Reinhardt
(Editors)

When Knowledge Sparks a Flame

Knowledge communication in the international
non-profit organisation SOS Children's Villages

PETER LANG
Frankfurt am Main · Berlin · Bern · Bruxelles · New York · Oxford · Wien

Bibliographic Information published by the Deutsche Nationalbibliothek
The Deutsche Nationalbibliothek lists this publication in the Deutsche Nationalbibliografie; detailed bibliographic data is available in the internet at <http://www.d-nb.de>.

Cover and content design: pooldesign.ch
Typeset: Hot Design, Austria
Cover picture: Dominic Sansoni

Translated into English by: Nicola Gander, Kathrin Bielowski, Markus Egger, Thomas van Breda, Paul Skandera

ISBN 978-3-631-56578-0

© Peter Lang GmbH
Internationaler Verlag der Wissenschaften
Frankfurt am Main 2007
All rights reserved.

Printed in Germany 1 2 3 4   6 7

www.peterlang.de

Contents

As a global organisation with more than 500 locations worldwide and employing approximately 30,000 co-workers, SOS Children's Villages is permanently faced with the challenge of optimising its resources. This involves the transfer of innovation and progress achieved in one part of the organisation to units located elsewhere in the world. At SOS Children's Villages high priority is given to knowledge communication - seen as an approach that strongly focuses on strategic and organisational development. After a short introduction on the history of SOS Children's Villages this chapter examines some real-life case studies to illustrate the experiences gained in the process of implementing and using knowledge communication.

The SOS Children's Village Manual provides a framework for our work in the field of child care in more than 458 SOS Children's Villages. Within a defined framework of principles, standards and guidelines our co-workers can make decisions independently in their own sphere of activity and act according to their own cultural standards at a local level. The implementation of this manual will be promoted through a well-organised process of knowledge communication on all levels of the organisation. Good Practice Workshops have been carried out in SOS Children's

Villages throughout the world in order to initiate a comprehensive exchange of knowledge and experience on the contents of the Manual. Furthermore, these workshops served as pilot projects for creating and developing a culture of knowledge communication throughout the organisation.

Tracking Footprints - Local research, global networking   79
Bianca Westreicher, Andrea Rudisch-Pfurtscheller

Tracking Footprints is a global project of SOS Children's Villages to research the experiences of people who have grown up in an SOS Children's Village. The project asks the target group to answer the following questions: How do you live today? Do we act in accordance with our mission statement? How can we improve our work? This article provides an overview of the individual steps of the research concept. The article deals critically with the topic of knowledge communication by examining success factors, learning experiences as well as the key challenges on the various levels of the organisation. Were the research design and the presentation of the results appropriate and efficient? How was the necessary research know-how developed? How was the validity of the research results guaranteed? What is their effect on the organisation?

Harvesting - Gathering experiences for dreams of the future   117
Gerhild Rafetseder

The wish to gather knowledge from our long-standing co-workers, preserve it and distribute it within SOS Children's Villages was what prompted us to organise the Harvesting initiative. Within the framework of intercultural Appreciative Inquiry Workshops participants were encouraged to exchange experiences, compare solutions and develop new ideas and projects. Participants discovered their own implicit knowledge as a source of learning and developed strategies to further utilise this resource and put it into practical action. By becoming aware of their own strengths and the possibility of using these in a deliberate, conscious manner, participants achieved a new, richer understanding of their roles as executives. These new insights also led to positive changes in their working environments.

In order to help children who have lost their families as a result of HIV/Aids
SOS Children's Villages is pursuing new avenues of care and support. The
challenge facing the organisation is to transfer existing knowledge from
well-established models to the right people in an appropriate way. The so-
called family-strengthening programmes were something completely knew
to many co-workers, most of whom gained their experience in the core area
of the organisation, namely in long-term family child-care. The concrete
task, specifically in sub-Saharan African countries, was to organise the
exchange of information between existing and future SOS Children's Villages
projects which were aiming to strengthen families.

This chapter deals with the extent to which profit-making companies can
adopt the experiences and methods of the knowledge communication
projects of SOS Children's Villages to optimise their own knowledge communication processes. The individual analyses of the projects carried
out by SOS Children's Villages emphasise critical success factors as well
as the unique operational and strategic competences of SOS Children's
Villages which made the implementation of knowledge communication
processes easier. An overview of the success factors shows what possibilities, suggestions and limits resulting from these experiences are relevant to knowledge communication in profit-making organisations.

On behalf of the children

Every child belongs to a family and grows with love, respect and security

With this vision in mind, SOS Children's Villages has been offering a very successful form of family child-care since 1949. Children are admitted to an SOS Children's Village if a return to their biological family is improbable or impossible. In the village they grow up with an SOS mother and siblings in their own house that is integrated into the SOS Children's Village community. In many cases, however, pre-emptive assistance can successfully overcome family crises and thereby prevent the uprooting of children.

The organisation has been growing steadily for more than six decades and can look back on a wealth of experience that is now being used to systematically further improve the quality of its work. To this end, knowledge management was established as an important cornerstone of the organisational development strategy and was also laid down as an objective in our five-year strategic plan. The extent of the challenge which we have set ourselves becomes clear when the scale of the SOS Children's Villages activities is put into perspective: approximately 30,000 co-workers in 132 countries work in 458 SOS Children's Villages, 359 SOS Youth Facilities and other SOS programmes.* They offer a home to more than 60,000 children and young people in need. Over 140,000 children and young people attend SOS Kindergartens, SOS Hermann Gmeiner Schools and SOS Vocational Training Centres. More than one million people benefit from the services offered in SOS Medical Centres and SOS Social Centres as well as SOS Emergency Relief Programmes. These statistics give an idea of the wealth of individual knowledge that has accumulated over the decades. They also highlight the importance of making this knowledge available to the entire organisation. The knowledge must be passed on suitably and in a way that is target-orientated, in order to create the best possible conditions for the development of our children and young people. If, for example, a youth project in a specific country has proven to be extremely successful, the knowledge gained from it should be made available to similar projects in other parts of the world, not least for economic reasons.

---

* figures as of December 2006

SOS Children's Villages can draw on a rich culture of learning and experience exchange on the basis of interpersonal relationships for developing and utilising its knowledge communication processes. This, however, does not rule out the best possible utilisation of modern technology such as the SOS Children's Village Intranet. In view of our worldwide field of operation, personal exchange is a cost-intensive process and thus not all co-workers can benefit from it.

Making use of the specific strengths of the different cultures with regard to the exchange and transfer of knowledge is of major importance to SOS Children's Villages. This approach has also been honoured externally, for example by the Austrian Ministry of Economics, which awarded the 2005 Austrian State Award to the Harvesting Project. The so-called "Knowledge Award" is an "Initiative for the Promotion and Development of Lifelong Learning".

Not least, the entire organisation received tremendous support and recognition for its work when it was awarded the "Conrad N. Hilton Humanitarian Prize 2002". This is the world's most important humanitarian award and is bestowed annually on an organisation that makes a remarkable contribution to alleviating human suffering. The prize money of one million US dollars was dedicated to developing new models for offering care to Aids orphans and supporting children and families whose lives are affected by the disease.

With its in-depth analysis of the resource "knowledge", SOS Children's Villages intends to provide a stimulus and source of inspiration to all those who face the challenge of implementing knowledge communication processes efficiently and in a way that is target-group oriented. All readers are invited to join us on our journey for a while, negotiating detours, one way streets and wrong turns to finally be able to look back on one of the most interesting sections of the journey in the organisational development of SOS Children's Villages.

Richard Pichler
Secretary-General, SOS-Kinderdorf International

Knowing how to know-how

Although trans-national non-profit organisations pursue different objectives to trans-national companies, the tasks they face are very similar. One of their increasingly significant concerns is how to approach knowledge. In the course of their history all organisations accumulate a large amount of knowledge which is partly useful and partly outdated but in any case mostly remains unarticulated and therefore unavailable to others. It is trapped in the minds of the organisation's members, in procedures and equipment, in behavioural habits and thinking routines. Frequently, its relevance, its topicality, its intercultural transferability and its partly imperialistic traits are not analysed. Therefore, organisations frequently observe two phenomena: resistance to the adoption of new specifications on the one hand, and all kinds of mistakes, on the other, which result from a lack of knowledge at certain levels of the organisation about the knowledge of other levels.

The SOS Children's Village organisation has set out to not only gather but also to revise its collective knowledge and develop transfer methods that allow for an agile adoption within new contexts, which normally implies more than merely documenting knowledge on data carriers. One of the results of this initiative is this book, which presents four creative knowledge transfer methods that place an emphasis on a combination of documentation and personal conversations. As the book shows, these methods can also serve as an inspiration for organisations in the corporate for-profit arena.

The first method presented in the book is the Treasure Chest, a good practice-sharing project which outlines how the participants of intercultural workshops worked on finding a way to best share knowledge. This approach facilitates the acceptance and transfer of the workshop results. The good practice experiences are documented structurally, in order to make them available to as many co-workers as possible. Furthermore, interested co-workers have the possibility of contacting the people who have either gathered or implemented the respective practices. The workshops gave the impulse for the establishment of a community of practice within which the good practices and their transfer are developed further. This approach does justice to the ambiguous and dynamic character of knowledge to a far greater degree than the one-time static and largely abstract analysis many organisations have attempted to implement with unsatisfactory success.

Tracking Footprints is a trend setting project which analyses the long-term effect of the organisational concept. Former SOS children look back at their time at SOS Children's Villages from a distance and reflect on its impact on their current life. This provides the organisation with clues on how to improve its work. Schools and universities, for example, could adopt these good practices very successfully and come to know how their graduates experienced the organisation and its usefulness for their later lives.

The loss of valuable knowledge that results from the termination of employment of organisation members due to retirement or other reasons is a problem companies as well as public administrations face. Within the frame of its Harvesting project, SOS Children's Villages provides its experienced managers with an opportunity to reflect upon their experiential knowledge in seminars and make their tried-and-tested practices available to others via the Intranet. The Appreciative Inquiry method allows the participants to establish a certain distance to their experiences on the one hand and to become aware of the significance of their experience and their rich implicit knowledge on the other.

The well-established SOS Children's Villages model alone is not enough to solve the problem of Aids orphans, since the number of children who need assistance is incredibly high. UNAIDS estimates that by the year 2010, 106 million children will have lost one or both parents. In order to be able to offer help, SOS Children's Villages has started to work intensely on col-lecting and transferring the knowledge and experience of existing and successful aid programmes. "Learning from one another," describes this knowledge transfer process the organisation has encouraged and initiated in order to develop and establish programmes.

The time is not ripe yet to decide whether the four projects, which were developed with a lot of empathy and expert knowledge on the basis of a participative approach and methodological diversity, will survive their pioneer stage to eventually reveal a positive impact. Due to the above mentioned success factors these projects are more likely to unfold a positive effect over time than many a comparable business project. The organisation and coordination of each of the four projects requires a lot of time and effort. People have to be brought together in specific places where moderated methods are used to involve them in conversations and encourage them to reflect and document, in the broadest sense of the term. Rigorous "cost calculators" as well as the managers of non-profit organisations who face increased pressure to operate efficiently might ask: "Is it really worth it?" If the currently available results are anything to go by, the projects have been well worth the effort. The future prospects of avoiding repeat errors and gaining efficiency alone clearly indicate great potential and real value, not to mention the gains evolving from an improved image as well as increased motivation and innovation. The critical criterion which also determines the possibility of a transfer to other organisations is whether the new knowledge culture is truly "lived". This ultimately depends on the organisational culture. If the norms and values are not lived, it will not be possible to keep the knowledge flow within the organisation alive. How to establish and cultivate a good knowledge culture is an issue that resonates in all contributions of the book. I wish you much inspiration and success in creatively extracting whatever is most helpful to you. May the reading provide you with new encouragement and ideas for your field of expertise.

Ursula Schneider
University of Graz, Institute of International Management

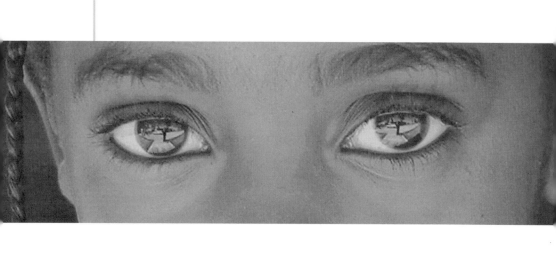

Astrid Brandl & Stewart Wilms

"Let the flowers grow"

Knowledge communication and organisational development in SOS Children's Villages

The founder of SOS Children's Villages, Hermann Gmeiner, used to say: "Let the flowers grow!" ("Lasst viele Blumen blühen!"). Flowers need water, nutrients and time for their growth. Without knowing it, Hermann Gmeiner had formulated a motto for knowledge sharing and for the development of our organisation.

Over the past six decades SOS Children's Villages has grown from the first SOS Children's Village in the mountains of Tyrol, Austria to become a large, multi-site non-profit organisation working in over 500 locations in 132 countries. A simple idea caught the imagination of a ready public in the aftermath of World War II – first in Austria and Germany and then spreading around the globe. All around the world national associations have evolved, inspired by the great personal commitment and pride of the founders yet deeply rooted in the distinct cultural and legal environment of each country.

Like any large multi-national company or organisation, we face the challenges and complexity of making the experience, the skills and the knowledge of people spread across the entire world accessible and usable for the whole organisation. Learning to do things better and more effectively is a key measure of our accountability. It is our responsibility as a company or organisation to share an innovation that has evolved in one part of the world, e.g. to save or extend resources, with other branches where this learning can be adapted, adopted or developed. Knowledge communication processes promote an examination of the role of the national SOS Children's Village associations, the central organisation and its branches. A balance has to be struck between centralised specifications and local autonomy to guarantee the best use of the organisation's resources in a way that builds on and nurtures the positive development of the work of SOS Children's Villages.

Between 1999 and 2005, we, the authors of this article, participated in and led various organisational development and strategy processes, gaining wide experience in bringing knowledge transfer processes and approaches into our organisation. In the following, we wish to demonstrate the relevance of knowledge communication for the SOS Children's Village organisation by exploring the history of the organisation's development.

Organisational development of SOS Children's Villages

The illustration below, which shows the four development stages of the organisation between 1949 and 2005, serves as a frame of reference for analysing knowledge transfer processes within the SOS Children's Village organisation. In order to take up the vivid motto of Hermann Gmeiner quoted at the beginning, we used the flower garden as a metaphor.

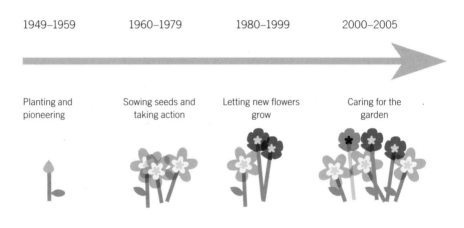

1949–1959	1960–1979	1980–1999	2000–2005
Planting and pioneering	Sowing seeds and taking action	Letting new flowers grow	Caring for the garden

Figure 1   The development phases of the organisation from 1949 to 2005

1949-1959: Planting and pioneering
Poverty and many war orphans and widows characterised the social situation in Europe after the end of World War II. It was within this climate that the SOS Children's Village idea fell on fertile ground. Driven by a passion to create things anew, it was put into effect with tremendous personal and emotional commitment.

As early as the 50s a presence was established in eight locations in Austria, Germany and France. Development proceeded step-by-step as more and more people became fascinated with the ideas of the SOS Children's Village founder and got involved. "Several German newspapers have stressed that only jazz concerts normally attract such crowds. A German tabloid

wrote that 'the Beatles on tour could not possibly arouse greater enthusiasm than a visit by Gmeiner'. Germany proved extremely fertile ground for the idea of SOS Children's Villages." (Scheiber/Vyslozil 2003, Tracing our roots, p. 185)

"Knowledge was gained through observation and intuition, improvisations and lonely decisions. On the one hand Hermann Gmeiner gave instructions in full detail, on the other hand he gave his employees large scope, great responsibility and possibilities to shape the organisation." (Scheiber/ Vyslozil 2003, Tracing our roots, p. 100f)

During this first stage, knowledge in the organisation was strongly characterised by the personalities of the different pioneers and was mainly passed on in discussions amongst themselves.

1960-1979: Sowing seeds and taking action

News of the SOS Children's Village modern childcare approach spread quickly outside Europe. Between 1960 and 1989 the organisation was able to build village after village, reaching a growth rate of 50% per decade. An action-oriented culture emerged within the organisation, aptly expressed in the words of our founder: "Don't just talk, do something". Within the entire organisation the optimistic opinion prevailed that everything was possible to help children who face a variety of difficult situations. Quick action was the norm. The services offered to children became more diverse and started to develop in a country-specific manner.

Further expansion began in Asia in 1963 with the establishment of our work in South Korea and continued in 1967 into Central and South America. From 1970 onwards Africa was the focus of attention, followed by Eastern Europe and Central Asia in 1991. The organisation did not originally plan to work outside Europe. This global expansion was driven by the needs of children all around the world and the interests of donors and governments.

Confidence in the organisation grew with increasing visible success. Government leaders and notable personalities around the world began to recognize the organisation, offering numerous awards and even nominating it for a Nobel Prize. In the course of the first 30 years the founding generation created a basis for helping children in need in 52 countries.

During this second stage of the organisation's development it became increasingly important to transfer more and more knowledge. At the time, however, this process was mainly confined to a network around the founder.

1980-1999: Letting new flowers grow

Famine in Ethiopia, ongoing wars in many countries and HIV/Aids affected millions of children in this time. The United Nations Convention on the Rights of the Child and a growing number of global non-profit organisations offered a ray of hope as they became an active force in society with increasing influence. While SOS Children's Villages continued on its original path, it was also engaged in an ongoing process of adaptation and development in response to the changing situation of children. Synergies were found in working with the respective neighbouring communities of each SOS Children's Village.

Starting with kindergartens and schools, and then medical and family programmes, a growing range of services was provided for the children and families of many communities. In 1979 there were only 43 of these supporting programmes in operation in addition to the 119 SOS Children's Villages. By 1999 there were already 594 of these in addition to 361 SOS Children's Villages. New, formal structures started to emerge at an international level, tasked with guiding the diverse growth areas. Guidelines, manuals and technological innovations started to be applied. The personal mentoring and verbal experience-sharing practices of the founding generation started to reach their limits and the next generation started to look intensively within and without the organisation for inspiration and learning possibilities.

2000-2005: Caring for the garden

Since 1949 the world has become ever more complex and increasing numbers of children face an uncertain future. SOS Children's Villages aims to keep its approach simple and focused on the organisation's core tasks while changing what is necessary to effectively implement its mission. Over the last six years the organisation has started to keep house well or, to resort to the flower metaphor, it has learned to establish an optimal relationship between the flowers, the garden and the surrounding landscape.

With the rapid growth of the past years comes the responsibility of making the experiences and learning gained in the first 50 years accessible to the entire organisation. Before 2000 most learning was shared through the aforementioned mentoring system, which handed down knowledge slowly from one generation to the next. As the general speed of global developments has accelerated, so too has the need to find ways of sharing experience and knowledge increased. The organisation has to learn to deal with its mission, strategy, good practise sharing and networks on all levels.

From an organisational point of view it became clear that the only sustainable path towards growth was to embed activities that were working well deeply in the national organisations. Over the years, several national organisations, primarily in Europe, have become financially independent. A growing number in the developing world are heading in the same direction with a 25% average level of self-sufficiency. Affiliation to a common brand and a set of strategies and organisational policies, paired with autonomy in operations and continuous advancements, provide a framework for the global development of the organisation.

How can we align our organisation's systems and the actions of its people in the best possible way to impact positively on the development of vulnerable children and families? This is where knowledge transfer can come in and make an important contribution.

The core competence of the organisation

At the core of our mission is the development of children and their families, and our product is, in essence, the welfare of children. This is easier said than achieved in reality. How can the impact of our core services be defined, assessed and communicated? Finding an answer to this question is a challenge we have to face. Since the year 2000 we have been digging to uncover and make the key tasks and competences of our mission transparent.

At the centre of our efforts as SOS Children's Villages are children in need and vulnerable children. They not only have a need for security, respect and a loving upbringing but also have a right to it. The individually tailored and family-based services offered by SOS Children's Villages are guided by the organisation's vision: "Every child belongs to a family and grows with love, respect and security". (Who we are, SOS-Kinderdorf International 2002).

The following diagram illustrates the vision, the mission and the two most important services of the organisation. The vision determines their orientation; the mission is their basis.

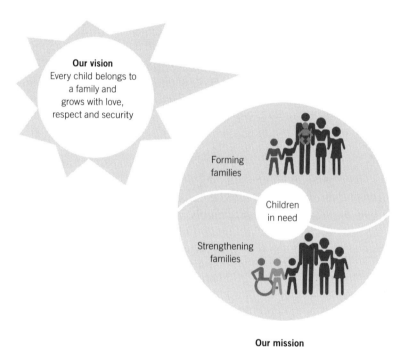

Our vision
Every child belongs to
a family and
grows with love,
respect and security

Forming
families

Children
in need

Strengthening
families

Our mission
We build families for children in need, we help them
shape their own futures and we share in the development of their communities. (Who we are, SOS-
Kinderdorf International 2002)

Figure 2   The vision, mission and two most important services of the organisation

In accordance with our mission of helping children in need shape their own future, two main services have emerged which reflect the core competence of SOS Children's Villages: forming and strengthening families. There is a strong connection between the two. Our priority is to strengthen the biological family so a stable environment for the child is maintained. If this fails, as a last resort, a new family is formed for the child.

Forming families for orphaned or abandoned children provides them with a stable home. These families, led by an SOS mother, live in individual houses within an SOS Children's Village. In 1949, Hermann Gmeiner established the four SOS Children's Village principles to give practical guidance in forming SOS Children's Village families (Who we are, SOS-Kinderdorf International 2002).

The four principles of SOS Children's Villages

The Mother: Each child has a caring parent

The SOS mother builds a close relationship with every child entrusted to her care, and provides the security, love and stability that each child needs. As a child-care professional, she lives together with her children, guides their development, and runs her household independently. She recognises and respects each child's family background, cultural roots and religion.

Brothers and Sisters: Family ties grow naturally:

Girls and boys of different ages live together as brothers and sisters, with natural brothers and sisters always staying within the same SOS family. These children and their SOS mother build emotional ties that last a lifetime.

The House: Each family creates its own home:

The house is the family's home, with its own unique feeling, rhythm and routine. Under its roof, children enjoy a real sense of security and belonging. Children grow and learn together, sharing responsibilities and all the joys and sorrows of daily life.

The Village: The SOS family is part of the community:

SOS families live together, forming a supportive village environment where children enjoy a happy childhood. The families share experiences and offer one another a helping hand. They also live as integrated and contributing members of the local community. Through his or her family, village and community, each child learns to participate actively in society.

Family strengthening is a service offered to families at risk of abandoning their children. These services range from family counselling and development planning to parental and job-related skills training. The goal is to help families help themselves, thereby preventing the abandonment of children.

Strategies as signposts

In order to strengthen our core competences eight strategic initiatives have been established to set the direction for decisions and activities until the year 2008.

Leading the way - long-term family child care
By 2010, 106 million children in Latin America, Africa and Asia will have lost one or both parents due to nothing else but the effects of the HIV/Aids pandemic (UNAIDS, UNICEF, USAID 2002, p. 1 et seq.). We aim to reach 50% more children in need of long-term family care and to establish clear and active leadership that builds directly on our core competence and responds to the needs of children, communities and governments.

Prevention – strengthening families to prevent child abandonment
In the least developed countries, 1.2 billion people live on less than one US dollar a day (UNICEF 2001). Children within this group face the highest risk of being abandoned because their families can no longer care for them. Through this initiative we will also directly confront HIV/Aids by playing a more active role in the community-based care offered to affected children and their families.

Increase worldwide fundraising
To continue expanding our international work, a sustainable network of diversified fundraising activities is being established around the world. One of our key objectives is to strengthen participation of all member associations around the world in fundraising.

International participation and partnership
Within the childcare sector we need to become advocates for our approach and participate in related debates. Also, as we begin to focus on the prevention of child abandonment, great potential exists for co-operation with other organisations that share our vision. Partnerships and international networks will also assist in accessing significant additional untapped financial resources.

External recognition of the SOS family child-care model and the SOS mother profession
Our approach to forming families in SOS Children's Villages is increasingly recognised by law in an ever-greater number of countries. Furthermore, if we achieve our objective of having the SOS mother profession included in national labour law, SOS mothers will achieve additional security and the profession itself will become more attractive.

Strong locally rooted national associations
National associations that succeed in developing their own local identity are respected as equal partners in society and receive greater local support. Associations that demonstrate strength on a national level, while simultaneously being part of an international organisation, unleash internal resources for the necessary growth of our work globally.

Research to state our results and bring innovation
After more than 50 years of working with children it is time to investigate the impact of our childcare approach more closely. Analysing the outcomes of our work is essential if we want our approach to be recognised by governments, international organisations and external experts.

Global human resources development
Our organisation must respond to changing donor trends, new humanitarian crises and innovations in childcare. Our ability to deal with these challenges largely depends on the skills and commitment of the thousands of SOS mothers and other staff working directly with our children. Likewise, the capabilities of the individuals leading and managing the organisation play a crucial role. Organisational strategies that build our capacity to learn, develop and work effectively are being put in place. These will support us in achieving the organisation's long-term objectives. Exploring and testing various knowledge sharing approaches is a key element of this initiative.

The stakeholders in our organisation

As an international non-profit organisation working in 132 countries around the world, we not only have to reconcile different interest groups, perspectives, requests, priorities and basic conditions, but we also have to consider the varied economic, political and cultural realities in the respective countries.

A short overview of the most important stakeholders[1] and their current requirements will illustrate this:

Children, who are orphaned or at risk of abandonment
Supporting the development of these children is the core focus of our organisation. Their voice has to be considered in all decisions that affect their development. Furthermore, a key challenge is to involve them in developing and continuously improving our services. SOS Children's Villages aims at spreading its services wider, while maintaining good quality childcare at the lowest possible cost per child.

Co-workers
"We need people who are willing to accept diversity in culture, religion and thinking, who are willing to accept other people as they are and to let them grow". (Human Resources Manual, SOS-Kinderdorf International 2002, p. 1). The questions that arise from this are: do we have the right people with the right attitudes in the right places? How can we use and develop our culture for strong strategically relevant performance? How can we infuse our people with enthusiasm for our core tasks, retain them and, at the same time, promote in them the necessary skills?

Co-operation with the communities
The SOS facilities see themselves as a part of the community in which they are located and share in community life. The challenge is to ensure that we have a lasting and sustainable impact in each community by working together as partners.

---

1   Stakeholders are the groups in the environment who have particular interests in the company's activities, or make particular demands on it. (cf. Probst et al. 2000)

Donors and sponsors
On the one hand, the large number of donors supporting our work allows us to establish a strong position in society. On the other hand, the organisation provides donors with an opportunity to donate and find meaning, thereby fulfilling their own needs. We always face the task of raising more funds in more and more countries around the world and allowing our donors to in-crease their participation as stakeholders in our work.

Other non-profit organisations which are active in the field of child, family and community development
International non-governmental organisations are increasingly influencing the development of international policies and legal frameworks in our field of work. Influencing this framework and obtaining international recognition is impossible without acting within this "international community" of non-profit organisations and international institutions, such as the United Na-tions and the European Union. To become more competitive in the future we must increasingly look outside the organisation to governments, the UN and other non-profit organisations and participate in selected processes.

Board members who voluntarily lead national associations
In each country our work is rooted in a national association that is reco-gnised by the respective government and has its own legal statutes. A na-tional board is established to govern the national association and make key policy and strategy decisions that shape the association's overall direction and development. As all board members work voluntarily, ensuring that they maintain and continue to develop a strong sense of commitment and accountability is a major challenge.

National governments
A first step when starting an operation in a new country is to establish a government agreement or ensure our work is in line with the national child and youth care legal frameworks. Governments, whose role as funding partners is becoming ever more important, are increasingly interested in participating more directly in child and youth care programmes, frequently offering monitoring and development services. For us, the most important

aspect in this context is the legal recognition of the SOS family child-care model and the SOS mother profession.

The chart on page 29/30 gives an overview of the role of the various stakeholders during the four stages of our organisation's development and the implications of knowledge sharing.

Stakeholders (as of 2005)	Planning and pioneering 1949-59	Sowing seeds and taking action 1960-79	Letting new flowers grow 1980-99	Caring for the garden 2000-05
Children - more than half a million	Focus on Europe after World War II.	Focus on Asia, Latin America and Africa.	Focus on Eastern Europe. UN Convention on the Rights of the Child agreed in 1989.	Worldwide. Major challenges: Family breakdown, child labour and child prostitution, HIV/Aids, war, child neglect and abuse. UN Convention on the Rights of the Child ratified in 192 countries.
Co-workers - around 30,000	Great team spirit. Unshakable belief in success. Enthusiasm and conviction.	Handpicked by the founder. Loyal and with little training. Natural authority and initiative.	Action versus reflection. Professionalism. Resistance to hierarchy.	Modern leadership. Individual development. Connection to the core.
Communities - more than 500	Active in 8 communities in 3 European countries.	Active in 119 communities in 52 countries.	Active in 293 communities in 111 countries. Urbanisation and technology.	Active in 515 communities in 132 countries. Globalisation.
Donors - in every country	Many private donors with small donations. Focused on reconstruction.	Urge to help children in need in developing world.	Critical attitude towards charity approach, community-based approaches are demanded. Help people to help themselves. Cooperation with big companies begins.	More and more companies and large donors in addition to private donors. New donors emerge in developing world. Donors want to participate in and see results of their contribution.
NPOs - national and international	Few NPOs exist, mostly church based. Start of UN and post-war NPOs	Many international NPOs are founded and gain more and more importance. Steps towards establishment of European Union.	Competition for funding. Co-operation in programmes. Administrative demands grow.	Influence legal frameworks regarding child-care standards in order to help more children at smaller cost. Cooperation and networking.

Stakeholders (as of 2005)	Planning and pioneering 1949-59	Sowing seeds and taking action 1960-79	Letting new flowers grow 1980-99	Caring for the garden 2000-05
Board members	A few committed members. Close to the founder. Donors on the boards.	Common values hold together. Identification with organisation.	Feeling of responsibility. Sense of national ownership. Participation in policy.	Balanced governance. Global strategic alignment. Local customisation.
Governments - partners in 132 countries	Political instability Austria and Germany occupied. Poverty, hunger in Europe. Partners needed for development.	Decolonisation. Donating land if no further costs. Industrialisation. Economic miracle in Europe.	Financial support for childcare. Monitoring of childcare. Economic unions form.	Recognition and legal integration of the SOS child-care model and the SOS mother profession. Funding and monitoring partner. Programme cooperation.
Implications of knowledge sharing	Observation and intuition. Improvisation. Decisions by individuals.	On-the-job learning. Centralised decisions. Decentralised actions. Network around the founder.	Start of nation-to-nation sharing. Spread of travel and meetings. Cost pressure limits face-to-face contact. E-mail and the intranet.	Stakeholder participation. Re-use learning across borders. Anchor key topics to the core mission. Basic resources for sharing. Learning and sharing from others.

Table 1:   Role of the stakeholders during the four stages of our organisation's development and the implications of knowledge communication.

Another overview gives a summary of the challenges posed by the various stakeholders of the organisation this decade.

Stakeholders (as of 2005)	Current challenges for SOS Children's Villages
Children - more than 500,000	• Further SOS Children's Villages • Further family-strengthening programmes • Guaranteeing corresponding standards
Co-workers - around 30,000	• Leadership development • Knowledge management • Improving co-worker skills
Communities - more than 500	• Local autonomy and partnership • Lasting impact
Donors - in every country	• Diversification regarding countries, types and sources
NPOs - national and international	• Lobbying for our approach and participation in discussions • Participating in networks and establishing partnerships
Governments - partners in 132 countries	• Legal recognition of our approach • Utilisation of our research results
Board members	• Strong local rooting and autonomy • Efficient leadership and management

Table 2   Challenges for SOS Children's Villages

In the 50s when the organisation was smaller and working in fewer than 20 countries a more centralised style of knowledge sharing and general management was practiced. Decisions were made primarily by the centre and implemented on the basis of many face-to-face exchanges.

Today the organisation is evolving towards a more federal model where national associations are legally and operationally responsible for their own work. The levers of control from a central organisation are becoming more and more limited as the number of countries and locations grow. As a result, setting standards for the administrative and programme areas, as well as for strategy development, requires significantly higher levels of participation. In order to guarantee that the decisions taken centrally are also acted on in each location, it is not only necessary to create a good level of shared understanding and acceptance but also to meet the desire for local customisation of services. This needs to be accommodated, while ensuring a general alignment with the core organisational mission.

Within our federation, knowledge sharing has become a tool in that it has lowered barriers between national associations and the central organisation and its functional areas. To use this tool, the central organisation has had to adapt its role from focussing on controlling functions to focussing on the facilitation of knowledge-sharing processes according to strategic priorities. The points that follow appear as the greatest challenges facing us in this important task:

Stakeholder participation: All stakeholders – from the children to our donors – desire and increasingly require more participation. Step by step this interest and energy needs to be harnessed. In particular, the unique experience and knowledge of each stakeholder is a vital resource for the organisation.

Re-use learning across borders: It is a key issue of accountability to ensure that learning is adapted and re-used across borders. Today's ease of communication makes it essential to introduce learning structures across the organisation that lead to savings and/ or better services.

Anchor key topics to the core of the organisation: Working across multiple locations increases the importance of anchoring key topics to the core of the organisation. The continuous development of a common understanding of the core of the organisation contributes strongly to alignment and successful knowledge sharing processes.

Basic resources for sharing: To cope with stakeholder needs and requirements there is a need to formalise some aspects of knowledge sharing. A simple level of systems and tools needs to be established and maintained without creating a large "knowledge sharing" functional area.

Learning from and sharing with others: Closer connections with other organisations enable experiences and knowledge from outside to be brought into the organisation. This can lead to significant resource savings. Almost everything has been tried somewhere else in one form or another.

Why was knowledge sharing introduced?

We have learned that letting the flowers grow is not enough. Attention needs to be given to caring for the garden. Strategies give a direction as to what type of flowers should be planted. Knowledge sharing gives that little bit of extra fertilizer and care needed to accelerate growth, mutual learning and development. As the garden grows and the number of countries we work in increases, the need to consciously stimulate cross-border exchange, learning and knowledge re-use will also grow.

As a global organisation operating in more than 500 different locations with almost 30,000 co-workers we are held accountable for optimising resources. With the ongoing growth of our organisation, complexity has increased and it has become harder to transfer innovations and developments going on in one part of the organisation to another part. Blind spots can form which often result in calls for more administrative systems to manage the new realities of a global organisation. As a childcare organisation it is imperative for us to ensure that every cent is invested solely and directly for the well being of the children in our care. To achieve this we have decided on establishing a simple, economical and people-friendly approach instead of developing our administrative procedures further. We have found that knowledge sharing processes and tools can help to cut some of the complexity created by organisational structures and administrative systems.

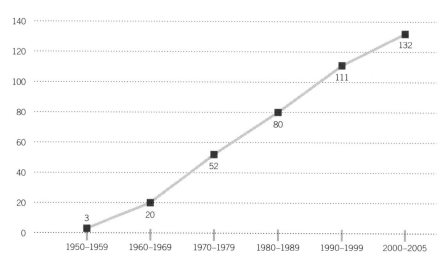

Figure 3   Increase in number of countries over the years

Within each of our co-workers there lies dormant a wealth of experience and knowledge that impacts the lives of others. Our co-workers carry this knowledge with them, sharing it when they are willing, able and ready to do so. We have retained a strong determination and dedication to supporting co-workers in their professional development. Also, as we are not willing or able to carry the substantial costs of high staff turnover, we are committed to working with and developing the people we have. Knowledge sharing is a key to connecting learning processes and motivating the current generation of co-workers. A strong intrinsic motivation and close identification with the organisation's core mission play a particularly important role. Leaders face the challenge of finding ways to access, release and foster this motivation.

Currently our knowledge sharing approaches are practised in strategic processes within specific projects and across functional areas. Our approach to knowledge sharing is anchored in the Global Human Resources strategic initiative, but is not a formal permanent part of the organisation's structure. This independence across functions and structures has been important, as effective knowledge sharing requires a cross-functional approach that keeps organisational strategy and development considerations in mind. Of course this can make things difficult as knowledge sharing processes can create friction within established management and organisational structures. When

brought to the surface and managed openly this friction can provide a further opportunity for constructive exchange, learning and development.

The following illustration shows a model that displays the three most important success factors in our experience.

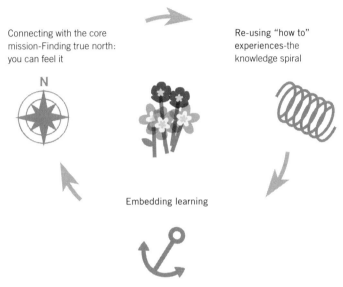

Connecting with the core mission-Finding true north: you can feel it

Re-using "how to" experiences-the knowledge spiral

Embedding learning

Figure 4   Success factors – Cycle of learning processes at SOS Children's Villages

Connecting with the core mission - Finding true north: you can feel it

Changes in the economic, political and social environment have forced changes on our organisation. The varying perspectives of different generations of donors, co-workers and partners have also driven change. We are told daily that we need to move quickly to adopt the latest fashion or technology.

If we, as a large organisation with complex tasks, want to remain on course in this sea of changes, the key to success will be to know our direction and to continuously return to the core of our mission. We need to link standards, strategies and other organisational developments more closely to the core of the organisation. The core can be defined as true north, the direction that pulls and attracts us and becomes our guiding compass. Experience has shown that the closer a knowledge sharing activity is to the organisation's core the more successful it will be. Our Family Strengthening strategy (cf. Chapter 4, Learning from one another), for example, shows that a strong willingness and motivation to personally engage in the process resulted from continually referring to the core.

Driving innovation will always mean finding this proximity and attraction to the core of the organisation, often in a searching and probing process that is strongly guided by our feelings.

A strong and simple foundation guides growth
The four principles established by Hermann Gmeiner in 1949 at the founding of the SOS Children's Villages were particularly compelling because of their simplicity and their clear reference to the organisation's core mission. The strong commitment of the organisation's pioneers to these principles enabled extensive and direct sharing and required few resources. In spite of limited ways of communication in the early years, learning around the four principles extended to all corners of the globe.

Over the last decade the four principles have been enhanced by the addition of 10 defined minimum standards that have to be met in each country. These well-communicated pillars, which are defined in the so-called SOS Children's Villages Manual, have likewise sparked learning and communication across the organisation (cf. Chapter 2, The Treasure Chest).

Soon after 2000 a strategy was formalised to establish family-strengthening programmes as a clear second priority for the organisation. Since the 70s this topic had been quietly pioneered on every continent. However, the initiative only really took off when the spotlight was put on it and knowledge sharing processes such as face-to-face exchanges (workshops and visits to other countries) were actively introduced, special knowledge sharing co-workers were appointed (cf. Chapter 4, Learning from one another) and clear standards for operation were designed.

Figures show that the family-strengthening programmes have made an excellent start and we can expect to exceed the goals set by 25-50 percent. This success was favoured by the conscious use of knowledge communication.

The upswing of these programmes in practice is due to their proximity to the organisation's core mission of child and family development. The programmes also allow for a large element of customisation nationally and limit the necessity for formulating detailed "how to" approaches centrally. The need for locally customised services and alignment with the core mission of building families is strong. Once these programmes had been endorsed as a strategy of action and then made explicit through the development of standards, growth erupted.

Attraction to the core is like metal to a magnet

Finding and keeping true to the organisation's core mission is vital for survival and enduring success. Innovations linked to the core lead to more effective results. Initiatives and topics close to the organisation's core mission generate a natural energy and alignment, which makes development and sharing quick and effective. The further away a topic is from the organisation's core mission the harder it is to bring it into the organisation.

The following four lessons we have learned should be considered when attempts are made to establish a link to the core mission of the organisation:

Organisational culture: Within our organisation we have a strong family-like culture. This deeply engrained culture is now also growing to embrace a performance culture. Stories and metaphors around family and family issues prove successful in this culture.

Endorsement of topics: We need to ensure that the topics are strongly connected to strategy, policy or other important areas. Without endorsement and management support we have found that there is little chance of an initiative taking hold on a global scale.

Successful managers have adjusted their leadership style: These managers promote common ideas and visions which many individuals share. This simplifies complexity, communication and knowledge sharing and creates an environment in which innovations and better care for children can grow. People start to talk about strategies and motivating standards. Processes like self and peer evaluation start to bloom and people focus on learning and improvement more autonomously. As a result, people begin to follow these ways of working of their own accord.

Organisational values can guide behaviour towards the core mission: The values and beliefs which made the organisation strong were made explicit through a global vision, mission and values definition process. We have yet to effectively use the values as a tool to create even closer alignment of our activities to the core mission of our organisation, but we have a strong feeling that they will play an important role. For example, our values of courage, commitment, trust and accountability are starting to be applied in policies and co-worker codes of conduct.

Re-using "how to" experiences – the knowledge spiral

Applying the knowledge gained in one location to another location does not occur on its own. In 1999 when we decided to introduce the concept of knowledge sharing into our organisational processes it all seemed so simple and natural. Six years later we can look back and say it was not at all simple. Connecting busy people in a busy organisation spread across multiple locations around the world is extremely difficult. Our discovery was that knowledge sharing is not natural. The hardest part is that you cannot see or touch what is really behind the success of some processes and the failure of others. Finding access to the implicit knowledge that is to be spread is a key challenge.

Re-use it quickly or lose it
Over the years, groups of people experienced in knowledge-sharing processes have joined together across functional departments, topics and geographic regions. People initiating new processes and topics got the best results when they consciously connected with people who had brought seemingly unrelated topics into the organisation. They spent time interviewing each other and learning how processes evolved and how future processes could re-use and adapt what had been learned. In the course of these communications, we found that people who had to adapt past experiences were also the ones who became the most proficient at extracting knowledge from completed processes.

For example, when we started the family strengthening knowledge sharing activities, the person responsible participated deeply in the evaluation of four other topics which had tested some element of knowledge sharing. On every international team working on a strategically important new topic one supporting, knowledge-sharing member was appointed. Ideally, this person had already worked on another unrelated topic and could bring in experience about how to organise sharing, feedback and development processes. Over time, a network of people with experience in some aspect of knowledge sharing has grown, leading to new and unexpected learning which we have been able to apply across management functions and topics. Investment in this cross-topic learning has led to significant resource savings on implementing topics globally.

It is easiest to extract learning when a topic is still fresh and the person or team has not fully completed their work. They are full of motivation and in the middle of reflection and learning. If a process lies too far back in the past, people will have moved on to other topics and the learning experience can become deeply buried or even lost.

After observing several interesting cycles of people connecting, evaluating, adapting and re-using experiences across topics we began to see this process like a spiral. Despite the time and energy invested in extracting learning, enormous resources were saved. From this, a simple working definition of knowledge sharing emerged: "People talk to people and share experiences and stories that help in their work".

Knowledge cannot be shared through computers alone as it takes the minds of two people in dialogue to share experiences. This person-to-person exchange can then lead to the re-use of knowledge, which is the most important indicator of success.

Re-use can focus energy, and chain reactions of innovation can emerge spontaneously. As long as the spiral is moving, guided with some conscious effort, new learning will continuously emerge.

Metaphors

In several knowledge sharing processes we have tested the power of metaphors and visual illustrations. For example, we showed people pictures of an elephant and a butterfly and asked them which type of organisation

they were most attracted to. When people described the elephant organisation they often thought of strength, stability, knowledge, memory and
clear direction. For the butterfly they thought of networking, creativity,
adaptability and a bird's eye view. Both pictures provided a good start
towards getting a sense of the organisation's vision, culture and goals. We
discovered along the way that building on simple metaphors is one of the
most powerful tools in knowledge sharing, helping to communicate complex ideas in a simple way. Metaphors make it easier to communicate,
share and, therefore, re-use this implicit knowledge.

Writing down experiences and good practices
New knowledge always begins with the individual. A master craftsman,
after gaining many years of experience, has developed a wealth of expertise
at his fingertips. But he is often unable to articulate the scientific or technical principles behind what he knows. For example, if you asked a carpenter
to write down how to craft a chair you would be asking him to perform an
almost impossible feat or your question might result in a 500 page manual.
Ask the carpenter to show you and you will learn the basics rather quickly
though (cf. Nonaka, in: Harvard Business School 1998, p. 21).

Our experience is that writing down good practices and collecting them
centrally for re-use has brought limited success. Writing things down is hard
to do and takes significant time resources. Furthermore, the people who
could re-use these experiences are often too busy to look for them and filter
through to find the golden nuggets which might help them. Rather, they seek
out face-to-face contact with others. In its most limited form this can be
done by email or on the telephone, but it is done most effectively when co-
workers are able to visit a location where they feel there is something important to learn.

What is important is that co-workers who wish to re-use knowledge
from other projects are able to seek out and find people who can provide
them with the knowledge they want, when they need it. Most learning takes
place in topic networks and in teams. We feel that team and peer evaluation
processes of various topics and in different locations also provide an important knowledge sharing opportunity. These approaches contrast with writing
down good practices and storing them in a centralised system.

Re-use needs an anchor

The 2003 strategic plan with its eight strategic initiatives was widely seen as a necessary learning process to prepare our garden for the future. Our limited resources required such well-defined and well-communicated plans. Today, thanks to the strategic initiatives, unanswered questions within our organisation about our direction and strategy have certainly been reduced. Knowledge sharing has also started to flow within the new networks and teams that have been established around our strategies.

A few supporting policy manuals have been developed since 2000 that capture our first 50 years of experience. In our project for the development of these manuals it was important to keep the total number of policies low. Previous manuals were cut down from about two meters of paper produced in isolation in various parts of the organisation to one box file containing policies that follow a common "mission and strategy" line across all topics. Of particular importance was the introduction of the concept of a "standard". The few standards for each programme and functional area provide quality measures to evaluate and guide performance.

Standards: highways for knowledge sharing

In the first 50 years of our organisation there were few policy or strategy structures to build on, other than the four simple principles of an SOS Children's Village. This lack of defined structures created uncertainty and limited the potential for collective learning. There was a need to have a few clear and transparent highways on which it would be easier to find, accumulate and share knowledge. The standards are the highways we drive on for good practice sharing. They attract our attention, guide our actions and provide a common frame for communication. When a need for a particular type of knowledge arises, we turn to the highway and are able to find people more easily who are driving in our direction. On the highway new knowledge can also grow more easily and there are many visitors who share our direction and experience. We can then build new off ramps and extensions to the highway.

Developing good highways is hard work and takes time – this was also true for establishing organisational standards. Having a longer and more participative development process ensured that their implementation went much more smoothly. It was better to spend more time discussing, planning and including people in the development and feedback processes than to rush to a quick result, which people would have rejected because they were not involved. The standards are supposed to move people to action and inspire them, not the other way around. Nobody should think: "The standard is something that was made in the head office to control us. We follow it but don't understand why".

In order to develop standards and strategies and accumulate good practice examples it is essential to record results, put them in a database or manual and then monitor and evaluate them in detail. This inevitably leads to bureaucratic processes. To avoid these getting out of hand it is important to balance them with people-to-people processes. (Cf. Chapter 2, The Treasure Chest).

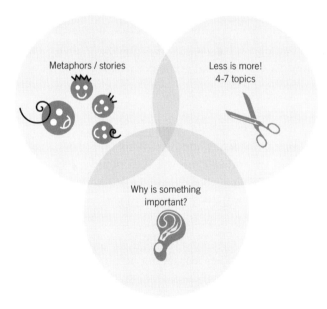

Figure 5   Lessons learned regarding the development of standards

The following three lessons we have learned have proven their value in developing standards. They also serve as good examples of cross-issue learning processes that could be established in the entire organisation.

Metaphors: Use a metaphor and/or simple story to communicate the key message. Complicated ideas are best understood through short stories

and pictures. People like to tell stories and tend to visualise well. Encourage a culture of little stories, where treasures can be found. If people enjoy this knowledge sharing method, the culture of storytelling will flourish.

Less is more: If you are defining quality standards or broad strategy themes for your work, less is definitely more powerful than more. From our experience, this approach is most successful when there are only 4-7 broad themes for an area. People can remember, internalise and work towards them without the need to consult papers and booklets.

Identify meanings: Start with communicating "why" the standard is important in an emotional way. Abstract, meaningless "standards" can become un-motivating rules that hinder knowledge sharing. People need to understand why the standard or highway is important and why they should use it.

By no means should good practice sharing as a means of clarifying the organisation's standards be used as a hidden control mechanism. Clearly separate good practice sharing from control and monitoring functions.

Embedding learning

Learning is about what you can see and touch. Knowledge is only brought to life when it is applied and integrated into real-life actions. This is a very hard "construction" job. Resistance is not uncommon and several adjustments may be necessary along the way. When the hard construction work is done the result will be general acceptance. New knowledge and learning will have been integrated into operational tools and translated into lasting actions.

We hear much talk about the need for effective implementation of strategies and policy across the organisation. Our approach has been to work to bring development and implementation processes together as much as possible. Development and implementation are not separate and must move together step by step. Just as with our standards development processes, we preferred to proceed slowly, ensuring high participation and tolerating some conflict so common understandings could be reached. The following examples have been chosen to clarify the relationship between development and implementation.

Building a profession for SOS mothers

In the early 1970s our founder became concerned with the development of a clear and strong profession for our core co-worker, the SOS mother. This topic was very close to the organisation's core and was discussed at the highest level, with decisions taken at a general assembly of all member national associations. Development steps were taken in many parts of the world. Today, more than thirty years later, building the SOS mother profession remains high up on the strategic agenda. Leaders across the organisation are still grappling with how to unify and embed this topic in the organisation.

Our experience shows us that the hard construction work of connecting some important topics to the organisation's tools, systems and structures still remains to be done. Important topics need to become a visible part of existing systems such as indicators, intranets and internal publications. Clear responsibilities need to be anchored somewhere so sufficient resources can be applied. Status updates and news on the topic need to be communicated regularly. If we are not forced to come back to these topics again and again, they are lost among the other urgent concerns of the day. In a large and growing organisation conscious efforts to embed topics are necessary to ensure success.

Simple tools can help knowledge sharing grow

In 2000 an annual planning approach and format was introduced across the organisation. A minimum level of written planning was established. This appears to have been a welcome movement as people were ready and eager to share their ideas, innovations and approaches using the simple planning format provided. The process to embed a planning tool was certainly aided by the fact that a written plan was a requirement for the approval of financial resources.

A year ago first pilot projects involving formalised planning procedures were introduced in the national associations. We were surprised that although only 25% of our associations were targeted more than 70% voluntarily provided plans. Plans reflected a significant understanding of and commitment to the global strategy. For many associations this was a first formal planning exercise. From these simple plans and the following annual reports, we are starting to capture and monitor global trends and identify

innovations and good practices which can be harvested for further learning.

Step by step, a simple formalised planning approach was brought into the organisation. The key factor was to ensure strong anchoring into the organisation's strategies and financial decision-making processes. With this came structural acceptance and almost automatic global integration.

Clear tools, like a simple planning format, have tended to accelerate learning and knowledge sharing. Put something concrete and simple in the centre of a learning process and people will have something to talk about and try out. In addition to planning tools we have had success with sharing knowledge through standardised child development planning approaches, an SOS Children's Village evaluation tool and performance appraisal methodology.

Good practise sharing and the intranet

It was extremely important for us to gain the insight that knowledge, unlike information, is always connected to a person. While there are very efficient methods to electronically capture and circulate information (SOS Intranet, data bases), knowledge, from our experience, cannot be effectively captured electronically (cf. Chapter. 6, Suggestions and recommendations for profit-making companies). We have started several processes to write down good practises in simple formats and share them globally via the intranet. The initial results of these initiatives are quite mixed. On the one hand we established a few new contacts between people. On the other hand the costs in time and resources to write down, store and share the results have been high. What is important is that people can find each other when they need some experience. We feel this is where the application of technology should be focused.

What learning do we take with us?

Our implementation of some knowledge sharing tools and approaches has been a rich learning experience. Some things have worked well while others have been less successful. We believe that this learning experience is valid for our organisation, but also for companies and organisations that face the challenge of establishing a cost-effective and people-centred knowledge sharing approach.

People-to-people processes are the first priority: True knowledge sharing only happens when people interact directly and when the knowledge gained is adapted to a new situation and re-used to bring lasting improvements. Anything else is superficial and will bring questionable results. The approaches and resource requirements needed for processes that do not directly connect people should be carefully considered.

Sharing, adapting and re-using knowledge is hard work: Sometimes knowledge sharing was seen as a threat to traditional structures. Real and lasting change means facing obstacles and barriers and finding ways to align actions. We have found that there is no one recipe behind knowledge-sharing approaches. It is a target that is continuously in motion, depending on the stage of development the organisation faces. Understanding this spiral effect and forming a network of people committed to this learning experience helped to make the hard work a little easier.

Aim to make it natural, self-sustaining and invisible: Knowledge sharing is not an end in itself and we view it mainly as a transitional tool for the fertilisation of an organisational culture where cross-organisational sharing and co-operation can grow. It is an approach that cannot stand alone or be structurally locked into one functional area. In time people learned that they could gain substantially better results and more recognition by sharing. It is particularly important not to keep on introducing unduly sophisticated processes or to over-promote the virtues of one particular knowledge tool or approach. We have succeeded in our task when managers start talking about how they could get better results by applying something they learned from someone in another location.

Find a motivating structural balance: As we grow, the forces of international centralisation push against the forces for strong national ownership and strong local autonomy and customisation. Decade by decade the num-

ber of facilities has grown and spread. A shift is emerging from managing decisions and developing "how to" approaches to establishing leadership in ideas and strategies. There is a continuous process of adjusting roles and embedding topics into the organisation's tools, systems and structures. With each step we need to find the approach that best motivates people in each location to voluntarily agree to follow strategies and topics of global importance.

Adjust, align and accelerate around the core service: Knowledge sharing is a tool to enhance and drive forward more consciously processes which are decided as strategically important within a large and geographically spread organisation. Individual or group interests need to be reflected on continuously and connected with the organisation's core service. The least resource-intensive knowledge sharing can then be achieved. If time and energy is not invested in finding and nurturing a close proximity to the core, the success of knowledge sharing will diminish. The organisation will also feel out of balance or 'wobbly' as a dissonance is created between what is felt to be the organisation's core mission and the topics that roll out. The long-term impact of not consciously aligning initiatives with the core mission can also affect such diverse areas as the brand, strategy and human resource development negatively.

We are obligated to not reinvent the wheel: management is responsible and must be held accountable for ensuring that useful learning from one location is shared with another. Processes and topics that are reinvented across locations are an unnecessary waste of resources. Also, ways of doing things that bring more effective results need to be shared quickly to ensure higher quality services. With the tried-and-tested tools available today there is a strong obligation to investigate and bring into place ways to embed knowledge sharing into the organisation. Failure to achieve this is a failure in meeting the basic responsibilities of a manager today.

The learning that is gained will be embedded into ongoing strategy, policy, human resource and organisational development activities. We carry the topic with us not as a formal and permanent part of the organisation's structure. Therefore, we do not intend to establish a knowledge sharing functional area. Rather, the knowledge sharing initiative should serve as a tool that allows us to look at processes and activities across functions, structures and systems.

Werner Hilweg

The Treasure Chest

Good Practice Workshops as a tool for quality assurance within SOS Children's Villages

"How did you manage to do that?" "How do you go about this?" Such simple questions at grass-roots level can gather considerable momentum for development processes within an organisation.

The basic unit within the SOS Children's Village organisation is the SOS Children's Village family. This is where we render our core service consisting of support for the development of the children and young people entrusted to our care into independent young adults, capable of living in a community. In their endeavour to achieve this aim, the SOS mothers and co-workers are faced with numerous problems and challenges in the every-day life of an SOS Children's Village: "How can I help this child in over-coming the trauma of having lost his/her parents?" "How can I succeed in involving my children in the decision-making processes?" "How should I deal with Franz who wets the bed?" "How does individual development planning work?"

Given that this type of question is usually of personal interest, SOS Children's Villages attaches considerable importance to finding "tailor-made" solutions to problems. Ever since the organisation came into existence, it has drawn on its wealth of experience of successful practice (Good Practice[1]) in order to guarantee and develop the quality of its work.

The international SOS Children's Village Manual, which provides a general framework for child and youth care in an SOS Children's Village, was published in 2003. It builds on the established, global experience of SOS Children's Village co-workers and on internationally recognised child-care practices. The principles, standards and guidelines that have been ga-thered in the Manual serve as a framework within which co-workers can make their own decisions and act at a local level in accordance with their own cultural norms.

A global project focusing on the exchange of good practice experiences was initiated in order to support implementation of the Manual. The aim

---

1   SOS Children's Villages has decided to employ the term "Good Practice" instead of the established knowledge management term "Best Practice", in order to counteract the common opinion among co-workers that there actually is one singular best practice that must be identified.

of this project designed as a series of Good Practice Workshops was to support the implementation of the ten quality standards outlined in the SOS Children's Village Manual and thereby guarantee and further improve care quality in the SOS Children's Villages.

Meanwhile, a number of Good Practice Workshops have taken place at continental, regional and national level. The results available so far confirm the positive impact of the workshops as regards a common understanding of the Manual's contents and the professional competence of our co-workers. Indirectly, this implies that the quality of the care in the SOS Children's Villages has improved.

Organisations or individuals who have responsibility for organising knowledge communication can utilise this project as a model, as a "good practice" for similar problems, as it were, or for optimising future projects. In this sense, the aim of this article is to present Good Practice Sharing in a comprehensible fashion as a quality development tool within SOS Children's Villages and to reveal that Good Practice Sharing requires an organisational frame of reference (in this case the Good Practice Workshops) if the comprehensive positive effects as described are to be achieved.

SOS CHILDRENS VILLAGE

Manual for the
SOS Children's Village Organisation

Starting point SOS Children's Village Manual

Imagine George, who is to be admitted to an SOS Children's Village somewhere in Africa. How does the SOS mother, the new SOS family, the whole SOS Children's Village community prepare for that event? Is an SOS Children's Village really the type of placement that best suits the needs of George? How can he be supported in building affectionate and lasting relationships? What are the minimum requirements of the professional and

human skills of the SOS mother so that she can meet George's needs? How can we best cooperate with the relevant authorities?

Imagine 13-year-old Alejandra, who for the past five years has been living in a Latin-American SOS Children's Village family with her three biological siblings and four SOS Children's Village siblings. Alejandra dreams of a future as a computer specialist. How can her SOS mother support her on her way there? What kind of support on the part of the village director and the co-workers can the SOS mother count on? How can Alejandra's desire for more contact with her biological mother be dealt with?

Imagine Peter who lives in an SOS youth facility in a European country and has started an apprenticeship as a car mechanic. Peter has difficulties in coping with the requirements. He is plagued by self-doubt; he is afraid of the future and often comes into conflict with his care person. What can be done to successfully strengthen Peter's self-esteem and positively motivate him so that he keeps going and doesn't give up? What kind of support does the structure of an SOS Children's Village offer?

Imagine Hong who has been living in her own flat in a large city in Asia for the past two years. Hong is a teacher and will soon be getting married. How can we use her outlook on SOS Children's Villages for the further development of our work in the future?

The 10 SOS Children's Village Manual standards

1. The SOS family child-care model provides a frame for our work
2. The SOS mother leads the SOS family
3. Children find a home in an SOS family that best meets their needs
4. The child's development is actively supported
5. Youth programmes offer self-development opportunities
6. Each SOS family lives as a part of the community
7. Funds and property are used responsibly
8. Planning and evaluation ensure a quality child-care environment
9. Each co-worker's learning and growth is promoted
10. The village director leads the SOS Children's Village
    (SOS Children's Village Manual, SOS-Kinderdorf International 2004)

These and other questions are part of everyday life in the SOS Children's Villages and ever since it came into existence SOS Children's Villages has been searching for, finding and giving good answers to them. In the almost 60 years of its existence, SOS Children's Villages has developed extensive knowledge and proven practice in order to meet the increasing requirements it faces under changing conditions. The target of the SOS Children's Village Manual was to structure this knowledge and bring it into line with current developments and future challenges. With the Manual, the organisation has defined a clear frame of action which, on the one hand, is based on its wealth of experience and, on the other hand, formulates future-oriented quality requirements. "We build families for children in need and we help them shape their own futures. We give children the opportunity to build lasting relationships within a family, we enable them to live according to their own culture and religion, and we help them to recognise and express their individual abilities, interests and talents. We ensure that children receive the education and skills training they need to be successful and contributing members of society". (SOS Children's Village Manual, 2004, p. 5).

The conceptual design of the Good Practice Workshops

When the SOS Children's Village Manual was released for implementation in 2003, one thing was clear right from the start: if we are to make a positive impact on the assurance and improvement of our care quality, it is not going to be enough merely to deliver the Manual to our co-workers. Successful implementation requires a consciously-planned implementation and support process.

Over the past years, awareness of the benefits of knowledge communication has increased significantly within the SOS Children's Village organisation. Thus, we conceived the idea of organising an international good practice sharing process for supporting the successful implementation of the SOS Children's Village Manual.

Good Practice Sharing - a method for distributing and propagating proven knowledge

We talk of a Best Practice when a task, a problem or even an entire project has been dealt with or even solved particularly well or ideally, so that the solution is regarded as a model (or a reference project) and can accordingly be taken as exemplary. (cf. Probst et al. 2000). The Best Practice Sharing method encompasses the processing, transfer and exchange as well as the further development of best practices towards optimal solutions for specific problems (cf. Reinmann-Rothmeier et al. 2001, p. 94).

SOS Children's Villages works in different places around the world while following one single aim. The experiences and insights that have been gained by putting this aim into practice have led to many good solutions and, therefore, suggest themselves as exemplary good practice examples.

Good practice experiences can be assigned to various levels and defined accordingly, as the following chart shows for the example of SOS Children's Villages:

Level	Example
Individual	When an individual has defined a good practice for himself/herself and/or applies it.
	For example, an SOS Children's Village mother who "swears" by her good practice regarding the family budget administration.
SOS Children's Villages	When the co-workers of a particular SOS Children's Village have agreed on generally applying a certain good practice.
	For example, all SOS mothers in a particular SOS Children's Village administer their family budget according to the same pattern.
National association	When the management of a national SOS Children's Village association has declared a particular good practice worthy of commendation or mandatory for all SOS Children's Villages in the country.
	For example, the national director of country X recommends that all SOS Children's Villages implement the development planning process for children in care according to a unified scheme.
Global organisation	When a certain good practice is applied globally throughout the entire organisation.
	For example, all countries with an SOS Children's Village apply the same proven fundraising methods.

Table 1   Scope of application of good practice experiences based on an example from SOS Children's Villages

The limits of Good Practice Sharing are determined by the simple fact that the proven solution "here" is not necessarily the proven solution "there". This is particularly true for SOS Children's Villages where solutions need to be highly individualised and where attempting to adopt the solutions on a one-to-one basis can easily prove to be problematic. If, however, good practice experiences from other contexts are reflected against the background of one's own situation and adapted or developed further where necessary, then the benefits of Good Practice Sharing are likely to be extremely obvious.

Good Practice Sharing as a part of knowledge management

On the basis of a comprehensive knowledge management concept, Good Practice Sharing can cover an array of important fields. Best Practice Sharing (similar to communities of practice) serves as a means of exchanging knowledge and optimal solutions and is, therefore, mainly to be attributed to the field of knowledge communication. Furthermore, Best Practice Sharing enhances the structuring and presentation of knowledge, experiences and procedures within the frame of exemplary solutions. In the case of successful transfer of Best Practice experiences and their utilisation in other contexts moreover, the methods employed contribute to knowledge utilisation. Ultimately, even knowledge generation is affected by practice sharing if the further development of good solutions is successful (cf. Reinmann-Rothmeier et al. 2001, p. 96).

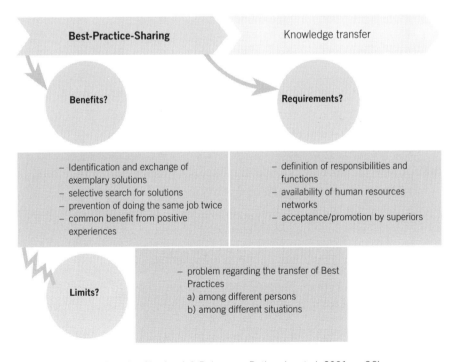

Figure 1   Best Practice Sharing (cf. Reinmann-Rothmeier et al. 2001, p. 96)

International organisations use the technological possibilities of the Internet and intranet for their exchange of good practice experiences. SOS Children's Villages employs computer-aided information systems in order to meet the demands of knowledge communication. However, an organisation such as SOS Children's Villages, whose core service is to build new and reliable relationships, also has a responsibility to guarantee a high quality of direct and personal interaction at all organisational levels. In this respect, SOS Children's Villages has at all times attached great importance to a personal exchange of experiences and knowledge.

The advantage of personal communication lies in being able to ask questions directly, thereby avoiding misunderstandings and gaining advanced insights. Moreover, personal contact enhances faith in open and constructive exchanges.

The design of the Good Practice Workshops

After the management decided that the implementation of the SOS Children's Village Manual was to be supported by an international Good Practice Sharing process, a planning team (cf. Hilweg/Lechner-Kreidl 2002) elaborated the basic features of the Good Practice Workshop design, which in its finalised version was presented to the management of SOS-Kinderdorf International for their approval.

The secretary-general of SOS-Kinderdorf International expressed the main concern of the Good Practice Workshops in a memorandum to all co-workers, "It is our avowed aim that all our SOS Children's Villages meet clearly defined minimum requirements in terms of quality for the benefit of the children and young people entrusted to our care. These requirements are defined in the SOS Children's Village Manual. The Manual reflects over 50 years of experience around the world and it will help to develop our young people, the mothers and the Village communities. In order to strongly promote the implementation process, there will be continental Good Practice Workshops".

The workshop design defined the following objectives which were to be pursued by the project operators:

- Provide a strong platform for sharing relevant experiences regarding the contents of the SOS Children's Village Manual.
- Promote a culture of information sharing, learning and innovation across the organisation.
- Optimise the SOS Children's Village Manual implementation process by developing a global implementation plan.

Four continental workshops were to be organised in Asia, Africa, Latin America and Europe with the participants being selected according to their future roles in the SOS Children's Village Manual implementation process as Manual Advisors or Good Practice Facilitators.

The Manual Advisors were required, preferably, to be members of the management and to be available as advisors or coordinators for the manual implementation process in the various countries and regions following the continental workshops. Their number was determined by the SOS Children's Village regions in the respective continents (Africa, for example, has seven regions). Prior to the workshops, the Manual Advisors' task was to elaborate an implementation plan that could be put into practice in their respective regions, and which, during the workshop itself, would be integrated into one common implementation model for the Manual together with the other plans.

In their function as experts on a particular SOS Children's Village Manual standard, the Good Practice Facilitators were required, preferably, to have a practical educational background. They were either nominated by the highest decision making body in the continent or via a selection process. They had to be available for follow-up workshops in the individual regions and countries subsequent to the continental workshop.

The following chart lists the responsibilities and tasks in the planning and implementation of the continental Good Practice Workshops.

Global Project Team
• Develop the global Good Practice Workshop concept
• Continuously update the management (principal) on the process
• Support the team building process of the continental workshop teams
• Provide the continental workshop teams with information, advice and the necessary resources
• Give feedback on the development and implementation of the different continental workshop action plans
• Participate in all four continental Good Practice Workshops

Continental Workshop team	
Continental project leader	• Develop the continental workshop action plan • Co-ordinate the continental workshop team • Co-ordinate and facilitate the planning,- implementation and finishing phase of the continental Good Practice Workshops • Continuously update the deputy secretary-general responsible for the respective continent • Continuously update the global project leader
SOS Children's Village Manual sub-team member	• Participates in the workshops as an advisor regarding the Manual content • Member of the continental workshop team
Action Researcher	• Responsible for carrying out an accompanying evaluation of the workshop process and contributing to the work of the continental workshop team

Table 2   Roles and tasks in the implementation of the Good Practice Workshops

The design scheduled five to seven days for each continental workshop. The venue had to be equipped with the appropriate infrastructure for approximately 20 to 25 participants.

Each continent was asked to consider continent-specific concerns in its workshop programme, while principally basing their structure on the following specifications:

- Introduce the development, objectives and implementation of the SOS Children's Village Manual.
- Impart knowledge communication methods, particularly taking into account Good Practice Sharing.
- Present good practice experiences, paying due regard to the SOS Children's Village Manual standards.
- Discuss the good practices presented and the further development of their contents.
- Elaborate a framework plan for the implementation of the SOS Children's Village Manual in the various countries.

An accompanying evaluation project (cf. Nguyen-Feichtner 2003) with regard to the quality and impact of the continental Good Practice Workshops was to investigate the following questions in particular:

- How, and to what extent, do the continental Good Practice Workshops support knowledge transfer and render themselves suitable for use as a model for follow-up workshops on each level?
- How and to what extent do the Good Practice Workshops support the implementation of the SOS Children's Village Manual and contribute to improving the quality of care given in the SOS Children's Villages?

Three different questionnaires were used as evaluation tools. The first one was sent out to the workshop participants approximately six weeks prior to the workshops for an evaluation of the preparation process, the second one was to be filled out by the participants on the final day of the workshop to evaluate the quality of the workshop process and a third questionnaire was sent to the participants approximately six months after the workshop, in order to record the practical impacts of the workshops. Furthermore, the Action Researcher documented his/her personal observations in a workshop diary.

The aim was to document the results of the Good Practice Workshops as comprehensively as possible. The primary goal was to compile the good practice experiences that had been presented and further developed through the exchange of experiences into documentation that could be distributed and used again.

In detail, this documentation comprises all the good practice experiences presented at the continental workshop, all input regarding knowledge management and Good Practice Sharing, as well as the general guidelines for the implementation of the SOS Children's Village Manual as elaborated during the workshop (implementation plan). Furthermore, it included the workshop evaluation report and the workshop minutes.

In order to support the comprehensive documentation of the Good Practice Workshops, a web page was set up on the organisation's intranet, which not only serves as a central information platform but also facilitates communication between the continental workshop teams.

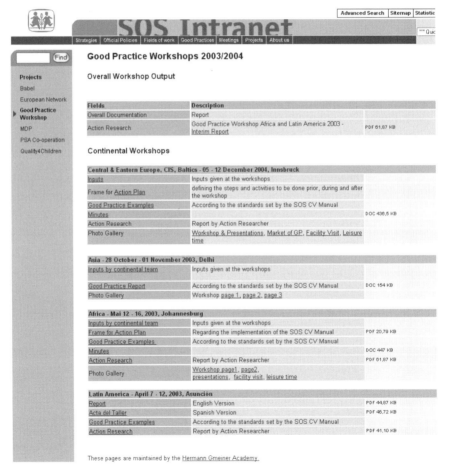

Figure 2   Screenshot of the Good Practice Workshop page on the SOS Intranet

From theory to practice

The continental workshops, during which 89 good practice experiences were documented, were attended by 94 participants from 41 countries. These figures alone reveal that an enormous knowledge potential "sparked a flame" that spread quickly outwards, as demonstrated by the array of good practice experiences represented here, emanating from diverse cultures and related to different issues (standards). The workshops also went into depth as regards the examination and further development of good practice experiences reported by numerous co-workers in a variety of functions.

The Good Practice Workshops were carried out in structured, separate implementation steps, which were predetermined as integral parts of an overall concept, but were open to refinement by individual participants. Using the Good Practice Workshop in Africa as an example, the core implementation steps and the results and experiences that were identified as relevant are presented below for each of the continental workshops. In some cases we have pointed out the distinctive differences to the other workshops.

1. Building teams
The four continental workshop teams were formed prior to the first planning meeting (June 2002), in order to offer them an opportunity to contribute to the development of the global Good Practice Workshop concept while still having enough time to plan their own workshops. The team members were relieved of some of their normal tasks in order to free the necessary time resources for them.

2. Planning the implementation
Immediately after the finalisation of the global workshop concept, the continental project leader started to develop the workshop implementation plan (see Appendix II).

3. Selecting the participants
Top management selected the Good Practice Facilitators as well as the Manual Advisors who were to participate in the workshop from a list proposed by middle management from the seven African SOS Children's Village regions.

By contrast, Latin America and Central & Eastern Europe/CIS/Baltics[2] selected their Good Practice Facilitators on the basis of the good practice experiences they had received from them and evaluated as worthy of commendation.

4.   Collecting good practice experiences

The continental project leader instructed the Good Practice Facilitators to collect good practice experiences regarding the different SOS Children's Village Manual standards from all the African SOS regions. Their investigation was facilitated by a form (see Appendix II). The good practice experiences to be presented in detail at the workshops were selected on the basis of the brief descriptions submitted.

5.   Evaluating the process prior to the workshop

Insights into the quality of the preparatory phase were gained with the aid of the first evaluation questionnaire. These questionnaires were sent out to the participants approximately six weeks prior to the workshops. Their analysis yielded the following results (cf. Lechner-Kreidl 2003):

The majority of the workshop participants were informed about their participation and role in the workshop approximately six months beforehand. The first contact was established via the participant's superiors or the continental project leader. Most participants felt very honoured to be nominated as Manual Advisors or Good Practice Facilitators. In their own estimation, the participants received sufficient information material to prepare for the workshop. They regularly communicated with the continental project leader as well as amongst themselves in order to clarify any open questions. Most of these questions resulted from the collection of good practice experiences.

The significance of good practice experiences was interpreted according to established definitions. "For me, good practices are activities that have proven good results and can be applied to similar situations in other countries". (Participant, Good Practice Workshop Africa 2003).

At this stage, the Manual Advisors were developing their recommendations regarding the implementation process in national and regional working parties.

---

2   Within the SOS Children's Village organisation this region is kept as a continental unit.

6. Carrying out the workshop

The five-day Good Practice Workshop took place in Johannesburg/South Africa in May 2003. A total of 21 SOS Children's Village co-workers, who were a representative cross-section from different functions within SOS Children's Villages, participated in the workshop. They proved to have been well selected for their tasks at the workshop. The main points of focus on the programme were to:

- Introduce the development, objectives and implementation of the SOS Children's Village Manual.
- Impart knowledge communication methods, particularly taking into account Good Practice Sharing.
- Present good practice experiences regarding the SOS Children's Village Manual standards.
- Discuss the Good Practices presented and the further development of their contents.
- Elaborate a framework plan for the implementation of the SOS Children's Village Manual in different countries.

7. Evaluating the workshop

On the basis of the analysis of the Evaluation Questionnaire II and the observations of the Action Researcher, the results of the African continental Good Practice Workshop can be summarised as follows:

The continental project leader together with her charismatic personality gave the workshop facilitation a special character. She knew how to mobilise each participant's potential for the benefit of the workshop goals. The co-operation and discussion between the participants was characterised by a strong sense of shared purpose, frankness and mutual esteem.

Out of all the participants, 27 percent answered the question whether the workshop fulfilled their expectations with "very satisfactorily" and for 73 percent the workshop was "satisfactory". In detail, the participants were appreciative of the fact that a common understanding of the SOS Children's Village Manual content had been developed, of the opportunity to exchange good practice experiences with other co-workers and of having initiated the Manual implementation process.

"The sharing of experiences reinforced my understanding of the standards".[3]

"The good practice examples were very good and very replicable. The outcomes were interesting. The network opportunity will be surely useful".

Out of all participants, 97 percent approved of Good Practice Sharing as an appropriate method for supporting the implementation of the Manual. Moreover, the Good Practice Sharing process itself was perceived as the highlight of the workshop.

"A lot of good and new ideas, new knowledge and opportunities of exchange and co-operation".

The main criticism was that not enough time had been dedicated to encounters and exchanges.

On a personal level, the participants particularly appreciated the opportunity to exchange good practice experiences with co-workers performing different functions and coming from different cultures.

«The different cultural backgrounds and skills of the participants had a positive influence on the exchange of experiences.»

The main criticism was that not enough time had been dedicated to encounters and exchanges.

On a personal level, the participants particularly appreciated the opportunity to exchange good practice experiences with co-workers performing different functions and coming from different cultures.

When asked what aspects of the workshop content they would be able to put into practice in their daily work, the participants specifically mentioned the good practice examples as well as the organisation of knowledge communication processes. The participants perceived the good practice expe-

---

3   This quote and the following come from participants in the 2003 Good Practice Workshop in Africa.

riences as either a confirmation of the quality of their work or as a valuable stimulus for adoption in their own working context.

Below, the approaches of the participants in discussing, presenting and developing the good practice experiences at the workshop are illustrated by means of the example of **co-operation with the biological family.**

Co-operation with the biological family

This topic, presented by Atika Jeddi, the educational advisor of SOS Children's Villages Morocco, is relevant for SOS Children's Villages, since in practice the children's relationships to their biological families are often disregarded and the children are thereby deprived of the possibility of getting to know and deal with their roots. The theory, as established in the SOS Children's Village Manual, however reads as follows: "The child's biological family is recognised as a partner in the care of the child: The child's biological family is informed about the SOS family child-care model, and is invited to get to know the prospective SOS mother and family of the child. They are consulted and kept involved throughout the admission process. This ensures that all the required background information about the child is obtained, and it provides a good basis for the continuation of family ties while the child is living in the village". (SOS Children's Village Manual, SOS-Kinderdorf International 2004, p. 28).

The Good Practice Workshop participant presented the aims for improving communication and co-operation between the biological family and the SOS mother, in order to support the child's integration and development. In practice, this has been implemented as follows:

- One social worker at the national office was released from his duties to dedicate himself to fostering the relationships with the biological families of the children entrusted to the care of SOS Children's Villages.
- The biological parents were informed about the child's development in the SOS Children's Village at least twice a year. The children are encouraged to write to their parents and visit them.
- The SOS mothers receive professional guidance in working with the parents and are offered opportunities for further training in this area.
- The biological mothers receive material and moral support.
- The biological parents have the opportunity to visit the SOS Children's Village on a yearly open day and are offered professional information on parental involvement.

The results showed that improved relationships with the biological families have a positive effect on the development of the children in the SOS Children's Villages. The majority of the biological mothers now visit their children in the SOS Children's Village. The SOS mothers, for their part, learn to accept the biological mothers; so altogether, the triangular relationship between the SOS mother, the biological mother and the child has been strengthened.

Following the presentation, this good practice was discussed in three work groups and proposals for its further development were elaborated. Those aspects the participants regarded as particularly important for further improving the already proven good practice were the truthful passing on of information on the child, the SOS Children's Village's openness with regard to a return of the child to its biological family, inviting the biological parents to festivities in the SOS Children's Village (e.g. Christmas) and ensuring that orphans, too, maintain relations to their former attachment systems.

8. Documenting good practice experiences

The good practice experiences in particular should provide the basis for supporting the implementation of the SOS Children's Village Manual and thereby supporting and further developing the quality of care given in the SOS Children's Villages. The documentation of the collected and developed good practice experiences constituted a core element of the workshop concept and was put into practice with the establishment of a Good Practice Workshop area on the SOS Intranet. Moreover, detailed workshop minutes (cf. Modungwa 2003) documented the further development of the good practice experiences presented.

9. Applying good practice experiences

Within the frame of the Manual implementation process, the different SOS Children's Villages decided which good practices they should adopt and apply. Since the number of good practice experiences collected is constantly growing thanks to the regional and national follow-up workshops, the SOS Children's Villages have an ever-growing selection of examples at their disposal.

10. Reviewing the impact of good practice experiences

The impact of the workshops on actual practice in the SOS Children's Villages was assessed on the basis of the results of the final evaluation questionnaire answered by the participants six months after the workshop.

The participants' answers to the question about what they particularly remembered from the workshop, can be summarised in three categories:

- Constructive co-operation and open exchange between the participants.
- The significance of knowledge communication for quality development within SOS Children's Villages.
- Expertise on how to successfully support the implementation of the SOS Children's Village Manual.

When asked about the impact of the workshop on their everyday practical work, the participants mentioned a better understanding of the Manual and increased skills, due to the Good Practice Sharing process.

> "It was very informative. It gave me good references, some of which I have applied or simply used to illustrate how things are being addressed elsewhere".

The participants were motivated both to apply and to benefit from the Good Practice Sharing method.

> "Good Practice Sharing is an easily comprehensible method enabling to focus again and again on the situation of everyday work and to exchange our experiences with others".

The supporting role of the Manual Advisors and Good Practice Facilitators in the implementation of the SOS Children's Village Manual was strengthened by the workshop. They themselves, however, criticised the additional workload these new tasks entailed.

According to the Manual Advisors, the frame of the action plan for implementing the Manual successfully provided a valuable basis for regional and national implementation plans.

The majority of the participants confirmed that they still kept in touch with each other, mainly restricting their contact, however, to co-workers from their own regions because of language barriers.

The contents of the Treasure Chest: Good practice experiences

"How do you go about this?" "Why does that work so well?" "What should I do in such a case?" - these are daily on-site questions. The on-site exchange for joint development of solutions provides an excellent opportunity for coping with the challenges of child and youth care. Communicating good solutions beyond one's own SOS Children's Village often renders a reinvention of the wheel and dissipation of valuable resources unnecessary.

Over the past years, the SOS Children's Village organisation has assigned knowledge communication a strategically significant position. It was, therefore, no surprise that the methodological concept of the project launched to support the implementation of the SOS Children's Village Manual was based on an exchange of good practice examples (Good Practice Sharing).

Up to now, four continental and numerous regional and national Good Practice Workshops have taken place.

Revising the workshop aims

To what extent have we been able to build a reliable platform for the exchange of good practice experiences regarding the SOS Children's Village Manual content?

The good practice examples presented at the workshops covered a broad range of topics and demands. They ranged from small, clear examples such as the effect of evening prayer in Indian SOS Children's Villages or the camping holiday undertaken by an SOS family in Paraguay to very complex practical experiences such as co-worker development in an SOS Children's Village in Zimbabwe or self-improvement programmes related

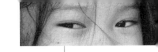

to young people in Lebanon becoming independent. Despite this diversity, the topics remained within the frame of reference of the Manual.

The exchange and further development of a respectable number of good practice example has "sparked" a great deal of knowledge in the participants and has enhanced their competencies as well as their understanding of the Manual content and has accordingly strengthened their skills – to the benefit of the children and young people entrusted to their care.

The second aim of the Good Practice Workshops was to optimise the Manual implementation process. According to the current results, this demand, too, seems to have been met. On the basis of the general implementation plans elaborated during the continental workshops, the regions and countries developed their own tailor-made plans. All of these included as an integral component Good Practice Workshops carried out according to the described pattern, thereby guaranteeing that co-workers directly involved with implementing the Manual have recourse to an ever increasing Good Practice Treasure Chest.

The third workshop aim was to support a culture of knowledge communication, of learning and innovation across the SOS Children's Village organisation.

The workshop results not only confirmed general and already known findings on knowledge communication but, furthermore, provided very special, innovative insights into the organisation of Good Practice Sharing processes:

- Co-workers do not only want to communicate their knowledge via computer systems but need personal and direct contact and discussions. For an organisation like SOS Children's Villages this is relevant insofar as its core service is personal relationships.
- The challenge lies with the structuring of the exchange process, in the course of which knowledge is communicated, further developed and made available for the use of others.
- The success of Good Practice Sharing largely depends on a clear definition of responsibilities and functions, the degree of mobilisation that has been achieved, the establishment, co-ordination and maintenance of the co-worker networks, the top-down acceptance and the support

the project is given within the organisation. In order to implement Good Practice Sharing processes, a conscious decision has to be taken after careful preparation and the necessary resources and general conditions have to be provided.

- It is advantageous to prepare the Good Practice Workshop participants for their roles in the workshop beforehand by, for example, suggesting they collect good practice experiences for solving a particular problem and/or reflect on the transfer of good practice experiences.
- The SOS Children's Village Manual standards have successfully provided an efficient and comprehensible framework for identifying and categorising good practice experiences. The more practice-related the questions to a particular good practice were, the easier it was to present concrete good practice experiences. It has emerged that those people who have developed and applied the good practice examples are also the ones able to communicate them most concretely. The most effective communication method is to interview the person who wants to apply the good practice in his/her own work context. It is advisable to subdivide more complex processes into various good practice examples.

Furthermore, it is important that Good Practice Facilitators establish and maintain networks (knowledge communities), in order to ensure the continuous exchange of good practice experiences on the core issues. Within this context, attention has to be paid to documenting the good practice experiences as a process in terms of a code of practice. A written summary of the practice examples was composed to give a short, standardised overview of the most important aspects, ensuring, at the same time, that the examples are easy to find in the respective database and other media.

The four continental Good Practice Workshops have provided a sound basis for a common understanding of the standards and guidelines established in the Manual as a framework for the continuous exchange of good practice examples and their further development. The results obtained so far prove that SOS Children's Villages would benefit from applying Good Practice Sharing unrestrictedly as a tool for quality development.

Appendix I

The ten SOS Children's Village Manual standards

1. **The SOS family child-care model provides a frame for our work**

   Children are given the opportunity to grow up in a caring and secure family environment and form lasting relationships. An SOS mother builds a loving family where children learn values and share responsibilities. She leads the family according to professional child-care standards and receives the required support from the village director and other co-workers, to ensure that the children's needs are met and their rights respected.

2. **The SOS mother leads the SOS family**

   The SOS mother shares her life with the children, offering them emotional security and the opportunity to develop new and lasting relationships within her family where love can grow. At the same time, the SOS mother is a child-care professional who co-operates with the other village co-workers in meeting the needs of the children.

3. **Children find a home in an SOS family that best meets their needs**

   Only those children whose needs are best met by an SOS family are considered for admission to an SOS Children's Village. The child-admission process ensures a careful assessment of each child before they join an SOS family.

4. **The child's development is actively supported**

   Each child is offered individual development opportunities tailored to their needs and potential. The SOS mother guides the development of the children in her SOS family. Other SOS Children's Village co-workers support her by providing services and organised activities that are not available in the community. All co-workers respect and promote the rights of each child.

5. **Youth programmes offer self-development opportunities**
   Youth programmes offer learning and growth opportunities and are part of each SOS Children's Village. Young people develop the attitudes, behaviour, confidence and skills needed to take responsibility for building their own futures and to become successful and contributing members of society.

6. Each SOS family lives as part of the community

Each SOS family lives as an integral part of the community and shares in community life. The child establishes relationships, learns important skills and develops the confidence to be an active and contributing member of society.

7. Funds and property are used responsibly

Administrative systems are structured to ensure accountability, while building a sense of responsibility in each SOS family and among all co-workers. The consistent application of these effective administrative systems promotes the responsible use of funds and property.

8. Planning and evaluation ensure a quality child-care environment

The quality of child-care is continually improved through evaluation and planning. Plans provide a clear framework for action, identifying priorities and enabling co-workers to approach their work in a confident and co-ordinated manner.

9. Each co-worker's learning and growth are supported

A culture that promotes sharing, learning, growth and creativity among all co-workers is nurtured. Individual training needs are assessed and the long-term growth of each co-worker is encouraged. Well-structured human resource practices help to build skills and lead to a greater sense of responsibility and commitment.

10. The village director leads the SOS Children's Village

The village director leads the overall development of the SOS Children's Village by promoting the organisation's values, setting objectives with his team, and ensuring that support services are offered to the SOS families. He guides all co-workers and plays a central role in guiding and promoting the professional development of the SOS mothers.

Appendix II

Time Schedule – Excerpt from the Action Plan – Continental Good Practice Workshop Africa (vgl. Modungwa, 2002)

What is to be done?	Time frame	Resources required	Respons. person
Include cost estimates of the Continental Good Practice Workshop in the Hermann Gmeiner Adult Training Centre (HGATC) 2003 Budget	July 30, 02	–	Thembi M.
Choose a venue and dates for the workshop	August, 02	Meeting with HGATC Management Team	Continental Team delegates Thembi M.
Communicate venue and dates to the Project Leader, BP Planning Team, and other role players	Sept., 02	–	Thembi M.
Send a draft action plan and time schedule to Project Leader	Oct. 01, 02	Feedback from Continental W. team members on draft action plan	Thembi M.
Prepare general information package & send to workshop participants – cc. Regional Directors	Oct., 20, 02	Time & names of Continental BP participants	Thembi M.
Compile a pre-workshop assignment	Oct., 02	Time	
Send draft pre-workshop assignment to continental team members and ask for input	Oct. 30, 02	–	Thembi M.
Initiate a consultation process with key role players in the region to draft implementation of a regional action plan	Nov., 02	Time	CV Manual Advisor
Start building up a network of potential participants for the regional/national workshops	Nov., 02	Time & e-mail facilities	CV Manual Advisor
Collect 3-5 examples across the continent of BP in the standard for which he/she is responsible	Nov., 02	Contacts across the continent, time & e-mail facilities	Best Practice Facilitator
Facilitate selection/appointment of a Meeting Organizer	Oct. 30, 02	Meeting with HGATC management team	Thembi M.

Hold a briefing meeting about the workshop with Meeting Organizer & other relevant role players	Jan., 03	–	Thembi M.
Make contact with other members of the Continental BP Workshop to share plans	Jan., 03	–	Thembi M.
Send formal invitations to delegates to facilitate visa arrangements	Jan. 3, 03	Names of delegates	Thembi M.
Apply for visas	Jan. 3, 03	Invitation letters	Workshop participants
Draft a programme for the Continental BP workshop in May 2002	Febr., 03	Input from continental team members	Thembi M.
Send final programme to Project Leader	March 03	–	Thembi M.
Communicate final preparations to workshop team members and workshop participants	April 03	–	Thembi M.
Hold a briefing meeting with HGATC team about preparations	April/ May 03	Time	Thembi M.
Confirm arrival schedules of participants	May 5–6, 03	Time	HGATC
Preparation of workshop venue & final arrangements	May 1–12, 03	Time	HGATC
Arrival of all workshop participants	May 10–11, 03	Transport, drivers, accommodation	HGATC
Hold Continental BP workshop	May 12–16, 03	Venue, accommodation and meals	Thembi M.
Departure of all participants	May 17–18, 03	Transport & drivers	HGATC
Draft action plans for regional/national workshops and communicate these with continental workshop facilitator	June 30, 03	Time, budget, transport, e-mail, other role players	CV Manual Advisor
Co-ordinate the CV Manual implementation process	2003–2004	Time, budget, transport, e-mail, other role players	CV Manual Advisor
Implement regional/national workshops, write reports and send to continental workshop facilitator	July 03– July 04	Time, budget, transport, e-mail, other role players	CV Manual Advisor
Co-ordinate & monitor the implementation of the CV Manual and prepare reports	July 03– July 04	Time, budget, transport, e-mail, other role players	CV Manual Advisor
Assist the CV Manual Advisor as needed. For example, give input on best practices	July 03– July 04	–	Good Practice Facilitator

Appendix III

Call for Good Practices Abstracts in Africa - Guidelines for Identification and Description of a Good Practice (cf. Modungwa, 2002)

Definition of Good Practices:
Good Practices are those practices that have produced good results in one situation and that could be successfully adapted for another situation.

It is suggested that the abstract should include the following information:

1.	**Name of SOS Children's Village standard:** e.g. The SOS Mother leads the SOS Family
2.	**Focus of good practices according to the standard guidelines:** e.g. selection, recruitment, training, …
3.	**Excerpt from the contents with a note regarding length** – maximum number of characters (600)

4.	**Why do you think they are cases of good practices?**
	• Briefly describe the reason for implementation of the above practices.
	• What were some of the problems experienced prior to these practices being implemented?
	• Briefly describe the impact that the above practices have had on the lives of our children and on the running of the village.
	• What were the processes involved in implementing these standards? Describe the tools, methods and systems used to implement this practice (please attach examples of these where possible).
	• How do the good practices that you are describing above address the following important areas of SOS (If at all):
	   – Vision
	   – Mission
	   – Values

5.	**Who was involved in bringing about these practices?**
6.	**Name and function of good practice facilitator**
7.	**Name of village & country**

NB. When you come for the workshop, please make sure that the GPs are on a disc or CD.

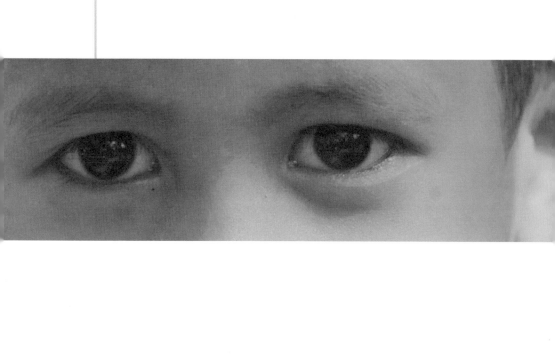

Bianca Westreicher &
Andrea Rudisch-Pfurtscheller

Tracking Footprints

Local research, global networking

Talking about our lives

"Life is not what one lives, but what one remembers and how one remembers it in order to recount it."

Gabriel García Márquez

"I am 24 years old, am separated from my partner and have one child. I completed an apprenticeship in hotel and catering and am now self-employed with my own business. I am not particularly happy with my financial situation. I find it hard to manage to live on what I earn. Splitting up with my partner was a very painful experience, as suddenly I had to look after a three-month old baby all by myself. Now I'm living mainly with members of my biological family."

I was 11 years old when my mother died and I came to live in an SOS Children's Village. I was happy there right from the start. I felt loved there, but it was still painful for me to have to leave behind the place where I had lived. I spent 9 years in the SOS Children's Village. I had a wonderful relationship with my SOS mother. I have fond memories of the loving atmosphere in our SOS family. We supported each other and the village director was like a father to me. I had no contact with my biological family at that time..."

Anonymous, August 2002

Tracking Footprints tells the story of those people who grew up in SOS Children's Villages, and who today have agreed to answer a number of questions put to them by the organisation:

- Does SOS Children's Villages act according to its mission, vision and values?
- What lives are the SOS Children's Village adults[1] living today?
- What were their experiences of SOS Children's Villages?
- What recommendations would they make?

---

1   For the purpose of this research study, those people who lived in SOS Children's Villages as children, and had left by the time the study was carried out are referred to as "SOS Children's Village adults".

- How can SOS Children's Villages learn from their experiences in order to improve the care offered?

Research means learning – learning by discovery. Being inquisitive – the desire to want to know something – is the driving force behind research, – and, of course, behind learning (cf. www.Tulpengarten.Entdeckendes-Lernen.de). Spending three years working on a research project that spans the globe brings diverse experiences as well as learning possibilities with it: lessons learned that are useful for the future development of SOS Children's Villages and also for the organisation's positioning. We were attempting to answer all sorts of different questions during our work on Tracking Footprints:

- How can we develop a research design for all the different countries and cultures we deal with that can be supported by all those involved?
- How can we achieve the greatest inter-subjectivity[2] in our research processes, thereby creating the fundamental conditions for the results of the research to be valid, when the research project is being conceptualised and carried out by co-workers from within the organisation?
- How can research skills and knowledge be developed?
- What format do we need to use in order to be able to explain the results and to communicate them to others?
- What effect will the research project have on the organisation?
- What value will SOS Children's Villages be able to extract from the project, especially from the perspective of knowledge communication?

On the one hand we have a mass of research results available to us based on the statements and recommendations made by those questioned in the study. This data underlines the aims and the quality of the work of SOS Children's Villages. Parts of the outcome motivate to continue working with

---

2   "Inter-subjectivity" means that a realisation is not confined to the individual. Instead, it means that other individuals come to the same conclusion having gone through the same experiences. (cf. Discussions on Objectivity, e.g. Jürgen Habermas 2003; Niklas Luhmann 2002).

certain approaches in the same way. Others open up prospects for the organisation to find out where there is room for improvement in its operations.
On the other hand, the research process itself has also opened up opportunities for learning, especially as far as the project management is concerned:
taking into consideration the particular challenge of having participants in
the study who come from many different countries and cultures and who
therefore have differing perspectives, which we then have to merge together
so that we can include their knowledge and experiences in our processes.

Firstly we want to show how important knowledge communication is
if you want to carry out such a complex research project as this successfully
with around 60 team members and 1,100 people being targeted from 20
countries so far. Secondly we want to work out how research results could
be implemented in the organisation, in order to be able to learn from them
and to set a process of improvement in motion.

Knowledge communication in a research project

There has long been interest on a global level in the life stories of people
who have lived in SOS Children's Village facilities. Various projects were
started here and there on a national level in a few countries back in the
1990s. These included, for example, Bolivia, Chile, Ecuador, Finland and
the Philippines. Research had also been carried out in the 1970s in a single
project covering Germany and Austria. However, it had not been possible
to achieve an accurate impression in the international context with the same
questions being asked of people who had grown up in SOS Children's Villages around the world.

An idea that was a long time in the making becomes reality

This idea was formally brought to the discussion table during a meeting of
the SOS promoting and supporting associations in the year 2000. The idea
was to gather specific information on the effects that the SOS Children's
Village work was having, in order to help the work being done with sponsors and donors. This idea then became reality. The secretary-general found

it was important to gather knowledge about SOS Children's Villages and its achievements to date in order to help the organisation to be able to improve in the future.

Eventually the Hermann Gmeiner Academy[3] was given the task of gathering information on an ongoing basis under the project leadership of Barbara Lill-Rastern. Tracking Footprints became the first long-term, international research project to be carried out by SOS Children's Villages with the purpose of gathering experiences from people who were not able to grow up with their biological families and who had first-hand experience of the care model in an SOS Children's Village.

The aim and purpose of the study

1949: the first SOS Children's Village is built. 2004: thousands of people have since grown up in SOS Children's Villages. How are these people living today? How did they perceive the time they spent there? What recommendations can they make regarding the standards of care given?

One of the central aims was, and still is, to draw attention to these so-called SOS Children's Village adults who are already living on their own, to show interest in how they are living their lives, to gather their recommendations and to learn from their experiences. This should result in the further development of the SOS Children's Village work and should show people from outside the organisation who we are, what we do and what we have achieved as a non-profit organisation. The results of the research should make clear whether our organisation is successful in acting according to its mission, vision and values. Furthermore, Tracking Footprints, as a global project, has also played a major role in building a global network within SOS Children's Villages. There are currently researchers carrying out the same work, asking the same questions and using the same tools to measure their results in over 20 countries on all continents. Their interest is in the development and improvement of our contribution towards a stable life for these children. This goes to show that world-wide research

---

3   The SOS Children's Village Hermann Gmeiner Academy in Innsbruck, Austria is a meeting and convention centre and as such a place of intercultural encounter and specialist exchange. It carries out research, analysis and contributions towards the future development of the SOS Children's Village idea, develops concepts to ensure the quality standards of the SOS Children's Village work and offers further training opportunities and counselling.

projects boost solidarity within an organisation such as ours, regardless of which world regions are taking part in the research. It also increases awareness of the network created by working together. It not only offers many chances to exchange experiences but also creates a solid foundation for each individual task.

Method

We have developed a questionnaire with both quantitative and qualitative elements as our research tool. The first part includes questions about participants' experiences while they were living in the SOS Children's Villages. The second part delves into how they are living today and their personal values. We also created an "assistant" to ensure that this questionnaire tool would be implemented in exactly the same manner everywhere. This assistant is an instruction booklet, the aim of which is to prevent any potential misunderstandings arising during the questioning procedure. As this study has to deal with different cultures, languages, social, economic and political conditions, the questionnaire is always used in conjunction with the assistant. This tool should ensure that questions pertaining to culture-specific subjects or questions dealing with the country itself are always dealt with circumspectly.

The interview partners are selected by using a cluster sample (cf. Atteslander 2000, p. 293). 60 people are chosen at random from each country. The target group is defined as people who are at least 22 years old, spent at least 2 years in an SOS Children's Village facility and left at least 2 years previously.

Framework

Tracking Footprints was carried out in 20 countries from around the world between 2002 and 2004. Over 1,100 SOS Children's Village adults were quite happy to take part in this project; they were glad to share their experiences, their opinions and their knowledge of the organisation with others during the project. As the average age of the participants was 26, and the average time they had spent in an SOS Children's Village was around 10 years, it meant that there were no doubts concerning the validity of their memories nor the strength of their personal experiences. This means that these people have a shared knowledge with the organisation and with other individuals that has resulted in a real gain for the organisation insofar as this knowledge and these experiences have been explained and interpreted in the course of the research process.

Over 60 project partners from various hierarchical levels, who all play varying roles, took part in the Tracking Footprints project, either in carrying out the questioning or in actually following up on the results.

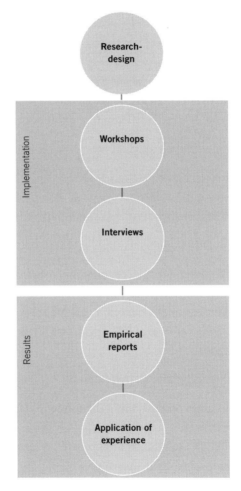

Figure 1   The Tracking Footprints' milestones

The project leadership team is responsible for the development and application of the research method. It is also the linchpin between all the groups

involved. The Tracking Footprints workshops are also paramount in linking all those involved in the project. Their main purpose is to prepare the project steering groups and those involved on a local level for the tasks they will have to carry out by ensuring that they all have the same level of understanding of what the research is about. Furthermore, the external interviewers are trained during these workshops. They then go on to carry out the practical task of questioning the subjects in their own countries. By including outsiders at certain points in the research, we are able to achieve inter-subjectivity and a certain distance to the SOS Children's Village work. This means that we are able to increase the value of the observations made during the research and it also means that the data we are gathering is more reliable.

In order to guarantee the principle of inter-subjectivity, we recommend working together with external research experts when evaluating the research data and to take advantage of their consulting services at the stage of implementing the study.

The philosophy of the project: Increasing awareness of participation
"Participation" is a generic term for the involvement of those at the receiving end, (cf. Lenzen 2001, p. 1052). This is an exceedingly important characteristic of the Tracking Footprints project.

We invite people to take part in our research who have experienced life in an SOS Children's Village. These are the so-called people "at the receiving end". Their role is to be the experts helping with the further development and improvement of the care-work being done. Our original idea was to have SOS Children's Village adults help with the development of the research tool. However, this proved useful only up to a point, as the project was so highly complex. For example, whilst we were developing the questionnaire, we did a spot test in Kenya where SOS Children's Village adults were questioned and asked for their feedback on the questionnaire.

Through dealing both with the questions that Tracking Footprints posed as well as with the answers given we realised that involving children and young people currently living in the care facilities in the further development of our care concept would be a useful tool. Our project partner's report from Cap Verde showed us that we could develop a living, learning tool which would lead to explicit local changes, "(…) the SOS youths' opinion is being taken into account in several forums of our region" (Dionisio Pereira, project steering partner for Northwest Africa).

The principle of participation had a far-reaching effect on the level of collaboration with the project steering partners. An international and intercultural network was created between these partners and the project leadership team. This network was active from the start, both in the development of the research design and in its implementation.

| Lesson learned

Although working together with the project steering partners on the development of the questionnaire was a time-consuming procedure requiring a lot of patience, it proved worthwhile as we developed a research tool that we could use world-wide

The design-development milestone: knowledge communication in a global partner network

The first question that sprang to mind immediately on assuming leadership of this project was what sort of research design we could develop that could be used in all the different countries and cultures and, at the same time, would be valid for all those taking part. We soon realised that it would only be possible to develop such a tool if we ensured organised and structured knowledge communication between the partners and the project leadership team as well as within the network of partners themselves.

One of the first important steps was to collate the existing research material from the countries in order to integrate the work that had already been done in those countries and to ensure that it was a valuable contribution to the project.

| Lesson learned

It was worth building on the existing knowledge base and taking into consideration research activities that had already been carried out.

We got in touch with the middle management and were able to put the idea of a world-wide research project on a firm and positive footing, as well as to discuss the resources required for this important partnership. Each of the managers was asked to name a representative from his or her region to act as a project steering partner and thereby to be responsible for carrying out this study in the countries of that region.

| Lesson learned

It was very useful for the project leadership team to hold personal talks with the decision-makers on the regional level. They offered the chance for the team to get a picture of attitudes towards the research project, to define requirements and approaches and to clarify the grey area between theory and practice. These were all valuable premises on which to base the tasks that the partners had to carry out.

The link with the practical work in the field

In our opinion it was only going to be possible to conceive, plan and carry out the study in partnership with our colleagues in the field. We needed the experience of those people who were close to the SOS Children's Village work and who represented different countries.

| Lesson learned

At first we had the idea of including another group of project steering partners, namely the representatives of the fundraising associations. They were to have the opportunity of bringing in their experiences from a marketing point of view, such as the type of question that is often asked by donors and sponsors. However, it soon became obvious that we had to restrict ourselves to a smaller group of "accompanying partners". If we had included another level in the project, it would have become far too complicated. It would have been very difficult to formulate clear questions for the research project had we included some very disparate points of view from the fundraising associations.

In the long term, our co-operation with colleagues in the field was to lead to a decentralisation of the research project. This would mean that in future the study could be carried out at regular intervals by the countries themselves. The aim of this continuing co-operation was to obtain relevant information for the project from the various working locations and the partners involved so that the needs and interests of their practical work could be included in the results.

The fact that the project involved the participation of so many people, gave us the idea of creating a world-wide network of researchers. The possibility was there, but unfortunately it only became a partial reality.

The greater part of the communication took place between ourselves as the project leadership team and the project steering partners. However, communication amongst the latter group was sporadic, "In terms of the communication amongst us, steering partners, I may say that, on my side, it has just been in the vertical. Meaning, I communicate almost only with the Hermann Gmeiner Academy. I personally think that we would have other gains with exchanges of information amongst ourselves, members of the team that are not necessarily from the HGA. It is a pity that I myself haven't done anything to invert this situation. It is also possible that, regarding the other colleagues of the teams, the communication is done in the horizontal, without my knowledge" (Dionisio Pereira, Project Steering Partner for North-west Africa).

Creating the maximum possible degree of neutrality
In view of the fact that this was such a complex, international project, it became abundantly clear that we required external experts to give their evaluation, and especially to prevent subjectivity distorting the research tools.

One of the methods we chose was that of the "critical friend" model. One method of reflecting on and setting ourselves apart from our own ac-

tions is to find critical friends with whom you can work together intensively. Being a critical friend means you have to ask critical questions! This method stems from the field of action research (…) (cf. www.qualifizierung.com).

The ideal partners for this were colleagues from the Hermann Gmeiner Academy and from the research team at SOS Children's Villages Austria. We discussed all the major topics with these critical partners during the planning stages of the project.

| Lesson learned

It was well worth continually including long-standing co-workers from SOS Children's Villages in the design development stage of the project. Their personal interest and experience with comparable studies were of particular value to us. This external input led to us looking at particular questions in a manner that we had not previously considered.

This co-operation proved that these exchanges were not just beneficial for one side only. All those involved profited from the process of information exchange and from talking about their experiences. Often these were just spontaneous exchanges during a working meeting. The project team profited considerably from the knowledge brought in by the experts. On the other hand, knowledge and experience that was gained during the Tracking Footprints project also flowed into the work being done in the projects being carried out by our critical friends.

Our partners, Bettina Hofer and Hermann Putzhuber from SOS Children's Villages Austria, describe the co-operation as follows, "The working groups offer the chance to pick out the central research themes of SOS Children's Villages and to evaluate the limits and possibilities of such a project. At the same time we can discuss the similarities and differences when dealing with international and national SOS Children's Village structures. The experiences gained with each research process and the exchange of feedback on specific projects are both contributing factors to the further development of our projects. They increase our self-confidence and our understanding as researchers and lead to an increase of inspirational changes of perspective."

Werner Hilweg from the Hermann Gmeiner Academy also had the following to say about this process, "I learned a lot with regard to professional project management. (...) investing a lot in careful planning saves a considerable amount of friction when implementing the project. (...) a well-documented project leads to clarity and comprehensibility. An additional benefit gained from this co-operation was that I was able to use many of the Tracking Footprints aspects in the development of the SOS Children's Village Manual."

In order to achieve the best possible inter-subjectivity within this research project we recruited another external critical opinion from the design-development stage onwards. Gerhild Trübswasser is an external consultant who has special expertise in intercultural research. She helped us, especially at the stage where we were developing the research tools. "I saw myself as a method consultant, in particular within the intercultural context, but also as a coach to the project team. Therefore, by going through each of the working steps together with an "external view" we were able to clarify the methods, which was of utmost importance. (...) Research consulting pays specific attention to the structural possibilities of reaching conclusions within heterogeneous conditions. It also takes into consideration all the different abilities on hand. In this situation, it is probably especially suitable for the framework of an organisation such as SOS Children's Villages with its world-wide work, countless cultural circles, social types and traditions, in order to maintain national and regional autonomy and collective principles. This framework was clearly visible in the project development phase with all its strengths. It was there both in the difficult repetitive search for a consensus as well as in the richness and variety of the solutions found."

| Lesson learned

As the external consultant was not prejudiced by internal knowledge of the organisation, her critical questioning enabled the project team to step back and think things through. This helped the team to see SOS Children's Villages topics with new eyes.

Helga Peskoller from the University of Innsbruck, Austria, was another external consultant, who helped us to create direct contact between our inter-

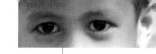

nal organisational research activities and scientific discussions. Here the focus was on the theoretical foundation of research statements, its aim being to support our presence in the "scientific community" through publishing our results.

Dealing with "the other" – cultural differences as a challenge for the project management team

A global research project means that different cultures and various framework conditions have to be dealt with. The countries in Latin America have a fundamentally different history of research to African and Asian countries. Where some countries can look back on many years of research experience, others have little or no experience at all. Some countries were quick to express their interest in carrying out the project, whereas others needed a good deal more time to prepare for the project. In addition to this there was the tension that can arise when different cultures come together. The job of the project leadership team was to find a common denominator for these varied prerequisites so that it would be possible to gather up the results from around the world. The priority was to create the same prerequisites for all the countries participating in the project. For example, we created a single questionnaire as our research tool to be used all over the world. Despite working closely together with the project steering partners, it was not possible to entirely prevent discontent. Those people who had already carried out a number of studies in their countries argued for a different focus in the research tool to those people who were asking these types of research questions for the first time.

At the same time, the cultural differences also became apparent in the formulation of the questions. One concrete example was the question about living conditions: whereas in one country the question of running water was seen as a central concern, in other countries the issue of greatest importance was whether the subject had a separate room in which to cook. As the framework of a questionnaire such as this is limited, we had to find a compromise. The onus fell on the project leadership team to ensure that everybody was aware of the global aspect of this research project. One of the central tasks was to ensure that not only was there understanding for one another, but also awareness of one another. A lack of interest of the groups participating in the project and the project partners would have hindered the success of the project. The decisive factor in creating intercultural awareness lies in accepting the differences. It is only knowledge and acceptance of differences between cultures that paves the way for understanding, mutual appreciation and co-operation (cf. Wulf 2001, p. 155). There were generally two possible ways of dealing with these differences within the research project: either to find a common denominator or to base the research on a heterogeneous method. Because of the task we were trying to carry out, we chose the first, even though it was neither the easier method nor did it help to avoid conflicts.

| *Lesson learned*

Today the project leadership team and the consultant, Helga Peskoller, are asking themselves whether, "this was the only possible (and meaningful) way, and what did we derive from it? Might it not have been better to start off with unequal conditions and then for us all to concentrate on trying to describe and communicate everything that was heterogeneous (on condition that there was an egalitarian difference/diversity)? This would have had the advantage that the way of thinking in the western world (rational, Eurocentric, colonialist, etc.) would have lost its predominance (…). The second method would have clearly shown the limits of understanding. Being able to describe these would have been a gain whereby that which was foreign would have remained foreign and distant, i.e. we would not have got used to it and neither would we have been drawn into it."

It was the secretary-general who asked for this project to be carried out. He described one of the most important lessons learned as being the realisation that cultural differences in the approach to the research project require us to show mutual understanding. This message meant a lot to the project leadership team as we realised we had support for the method we had chosen. However, during the project development phase, it became one of the greatest challenges for the decision makers from all the hierarchical levels to respect the points of view of other "colleagues" and to put their own interests on hold in favour of finding a consensus for all the cultural backgrounds and continents involved in the project.

Resume I: The main consequences for knowledge communication

The multitude and diversity of the project partners, the cultures, as well as the internal and external organisational levels present a great challenge for communication and co-ordination. This is especially the case as there is a requirement that the research concept should be accepted by all those taking part so that the project can be carried out successfully. In order to fulfil this requirement, we had to take into account the differing points of view of our partners when we were developing the design. We also had to make them aware that they were going to be responsible for the success of this project. Another factor was that most of the communication between the internal organisation partners was mainly through the medium of Internet and e-mail. There was only a limited possibility of holding personal meetings. This made it difficult to "develop a communal" research design.

The points of view from people outside the organisation were, and still are, very important for us. They helped us achieve inter-subjectivity in our research process and to make strong arguments for the results of our project. At the same time they allowed us access to experience and knowledge from outside the organisation. All in all, these methods led to us having a wide spectrum of knowledge communication in the project.

The implementation milestone: of asking and being asked

Seven countries in Latin America, Africa, Asia and Europe were the first in which the Tracking Footprints project was carried out. They all fulfilled the criteria that had been defined in the research design, which amongst other things included: how long the SOS Children's Village work had been carried out in that country (approx. 20 years so that there would be enough SOS Children's Village adults available); knowing where the SOS Children's Village adults were now living and being able to contact them; a good while since other interviews had been carried out with SOS Children's Village adults (at least six months), so that they would not get fed up with being asked questions again.

The project steering team had to set up a suitable communication network. This was the pioneering work they carried out (cf. Figure 2). The task was to find SOS Children's Village co-workers in each country who would be responsible for the project. Their main tasks were: to collate an address list of the people in the target group for the sample survey; to get in touch with potential interview partners and to tell them about the research project. External interviewers had to be found and to be trained to carry out the interviews.

The interviewers played a very important role in carrying out this study. It was therefore of paramount importance that they were well prepared before carrying out the interview. They had to be chosen with care and consideration. They needed to have actual previous experience in and knowledge of carrying out similar interviews. They also had to be reliable. Both men and women were needed to carry out the job and they had to be about the same age or older than those people being questioned.

Because we wanted to achieve a research-orientated project and maximise the objectivity of our procedures, it was important to find interviewers who came from outside the SOS Children's Village structure. The external partners could either have been students who had almost completed their degree (preferably from the social sciences) or freelance researchers.

It proved valuable to use contacts with whom we had previously worked. For example from universities, private research facilities or consultancy firms.

Finally we had to integrate the real protagonists into the network of the project, namely the SOS Children's Village adults (target group) who were going to be interviewed.

During this phase the project steering partners were in constant touch with the project leadership team who were co-ordinating the preparations on a global level. One of the milestones of this phase was the Tracking Footprints workshop.

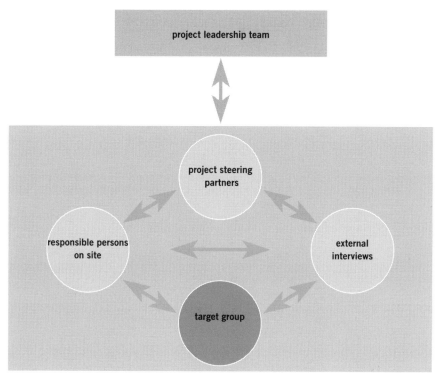

Figure 2   Communication network in the implementation phase

Tracking Footprints workshops as a platform for building competencies and exchanging

One of the direct consultancy and accompanying services offered by the project leadership team during the first years of the project was to offer workshops in those countries where the study was going to be carried out. The aim of these workshops was to familiarise the local project steering partners with the research procedures, to discuss relevant topics and to prepare them for carrying out the project. One of the most important elements was to create comparable conditions both in an international and intercultural context, above all, for the interview settings and the application of the questionnaire.

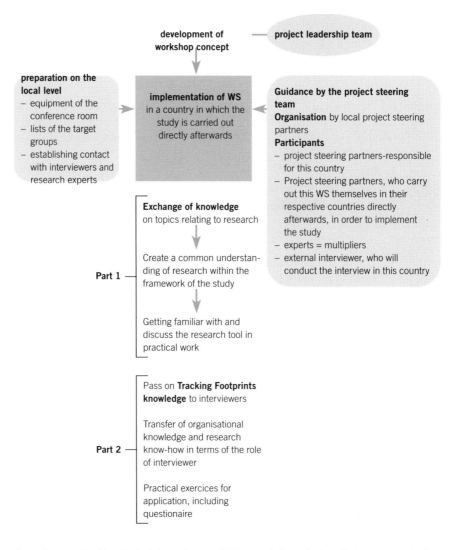

Figure 3   Tracking Footprints workshops (WS) as a platform for knowledge communication

The workshops were planned for two target groups. The first round was held only for the project steering partners or those people who were responsible for the project on a national level. The aim was to allow them to deal with questions about the theory and practice of Tracking Footprints. Through this medium we wanted everybody involved to take on more responsibility for carrying out the study in their countries.

Following on from this there was a second round of workshops. These were held primarily for the external interviewers. Here we dealt with the theoretical basis on the one hand and with tangible, practical exercises on the other: the interviewers were trained for their future roles and also on how to implement the questionnaire. They were given information about their client, SOS Children's Villages, and about the research project. The project steering partners were also invited to these workshops so that they could see how the interviewers were being prepared with the view of being able to use these methods in their own work (cf. Figure 3, p. 102).

The project steering partners who had already gained experience in implementing Tracking Footprints were asked to take part in the workshops as experts, in order to be able to share their knowledge and experiences with the other participants.

Lesson learned

This development could be seen as making a contribution to the promotion and motivation of co-workers. It was not conceived as such, but nevertheless, it turned out, here and there, as an added and unexpected effect. This process had not been envisaged as leading to developments such as gaining a promotion in terms of hierarchy. Far more, they were intended to give a quantitative extension of tasks, taking into account the diversity of the actions involved, or as a "job enrichment" i.e. a qualitative extension of the tasks in view of the decision making process and room for control involved (cf. Reinmann-Rothmeier et al. 2001, p. 119).

The example of the project steering partner for Northwest Africa shows such a development. In addition to his leading function on a national level he also took on the role of a multiplier on an international level. He wrote about this, "Acting as a multiplier is something that gives me incentive, in this pioneer project (…) so that I was ready to do whatever I can to implement the project and its spirit in all the countries in the daily routine (...) of our SOS Children's Villages." (Dionisio Pereira, 2005, project steering partner for Northwest Africa)

The project steering partners were given the workshop concepts to work with. They used these concepts in their own countries to help them prepare the local participants to carry out the study. This meant that the research concept and the questionnaire were implemented as homogenously as possible on an international level.

| Lesson learned

The workshops were generally welcomed by the project steering partners and seen to be an important step in professionalising the study by being able to exchange experience: «Partager avec les autres pays qu'ils aient ou non déjà initié l'étude est nécessaire afin de bénéficier de nos expériences mutuelles et éviter d'éventuels problèmes. D'ailleurs, j'ai moi-même bénéficié de l'expérience pilote du Kenya (...) à l'occasion du workshop à Casablanca» (Atika Baghdad, 2005, project steering parnter for North Africa).

The project steering partner for Central and West Africa with an external interviewer, practicing an interview situation during the Tracking Footprints workshop in Morocco.

As far as carrying out the interviews was concerned, people were, in general, very happy to take part and, at the same time, highly motivated to be an interview partner. The most important factor here was that they all took part voluntarily, "The general impression we got by conducting interviews was that most of the interview partners (more than 75%) took part in the survey with enthusiasm" (Report Sheet Sri Lanka 2002).

Lesson learned

It was obvious that the principle of using volunteers increased the participational motivation

---

Resume II: Main consequences for knowledge communication

The network of project participants increased greatly and became far more complex during the research process phase. At the same time many challenges and tasks arose concerning knowledge communication that made it unthinkable that participants would not meet personally and work together in the same place. Primarily, this concerned gathering input from the SOS Children's Village adults. We were convinced that asking the participants the questions in an interview situation would lead to them telling us far more than if they were just handed the questionnaires to fill out on their own. It was equally unthinkable that we would not work together personally with the co-workers who were to carry out the interviews. It was necessary to develop their competencies, not only in the theory of social research knowledge, but also to allow them to think about social competences and how to deal with interview partners in an interview situation.

Knowledge communication in the organisation

Once the interviews had been completed, the questionnaires were returned to the people in charge of the project locally where they were evaluated by experts. The excitement mounted: what would the SOS Children's Village adults have to report? Would they support the care concept and methods used in the SOS Children's Villages? On the one hand we were nervous that the results we received might not be the best for our fundraising requirements and might tarnish the positive self-image of the organisation that we have. On the other hand we were still very interested in learning from the people concerned in order to further develop the SOS Children's Village work and to meet the needs of the children in our care. Even the decision-makers were clear on the point that none of the statements from those interviewed, whether "positive or negative," should be swept under the carpet: they should not be concealed from the public, nor the SOS Children's Village co-workers, nor the SOS Children's Village children or the young adults.

The following questions arose concerning how to deal with the research results we had gathered:

- What will the fundamental reaction of the organisation be to the outcome – whether positive or negative?
- How will we communicate the results of the research project and to whom?
- How will the organisation use the results for public relations, the practical SOS Children's Village work and for training concepts in the fields of quality assurance and development?

An appreciative attitude towards the knowledge gained from Tracking Footprints underlies the project. Knowledge communication means much more than the mere transfer of information; it does not only concern the "where", "when" and "what" (cf. Reinhardt 2004, p. 3).

The mere exchange of information is the reverse of the swapping of experiences, realisations, opinions, values and ideals, the efficient use of knowledge gained through experience and the implicit knowledge of the

research project. In general, any knowledge gained through experience will be seen as an increasingly important organisational and company resource. This knowledge gained from experience has to be transferred along with the more basic transfer of information. It needs to be made attainable and transferable: This successful/critical resource can only be accessed by a few people apart from the person who has gained the experience. It is very complicated to communicate this knowledge as the experience is always tied to the individual's background of experience, (cf. Reinhardt 2004, p. 33).

This quandary is also true of Tracking Footprints. The project leadership, with its distance from the practical work in the field, had particular problems with implementing the research design because of the knowledge gap here. In this phase the project steering partners and the people they worked together with were those who were gaining experience.

Reporting on knowledge

The idea of having report sheets was born. Guide questions were sent out to the project steering partners with which they could document the research process and which made it possible for them to exchange knowledge gained from their experience. This document not only helped them to reflect on their work, but was also sent back to the project leadership team.

| Extract from the report sheets - some of the guide questions

- What difficulties presented themselves whilst compiling the list of SOS Children's Village adults?
- How were the external interviewers chosen?
- How was contact made with potential interview partners?
- What problems and difficulties arose when carrying out the interviews?
- etc.

In future this documentation will serve as the basis for the development of research concepts in long-term research projects within the organisation.

We did not make the report sheets available to all our project steering partners. This meant that we did not support the direct transfer of knowledge and experience. If we had distributed these documents to everybody, it would not only have enlivened the above-mentioned network, but would also have made everybody more aware of the fact that similar learning experiences could be swapped and used amongst the group

The report sheets emphasised the knowledge gained through experience during the interview phase.

The knowledge reflected in the research results themselves (Figure 4), was compiled into a national result report in each of the countries by research experts and sent to the project leadership team. Sending out the research results was the first step taken towards the communication of knowledge amongst all the countries. The project leadership team was responsible for compiling all the data. The result was the first global research report within the SOS Children's Village organisation. The team not only worked out trends and recommendations for future use of the research results, but also described the values and attitudes that underpinned the whole process.

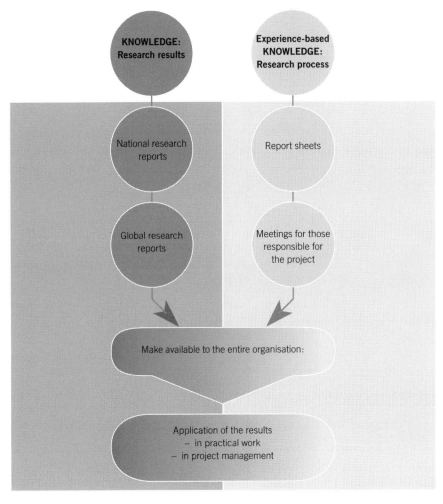

Does SOS Children's Villages act in accordance with its guidelines? –
Relevant research results

We had a wealth of research results that were based on the statements, experiences and recommendations of the interview partners (cf. Pittracher, Rudisch-Pfurtscheller, Westreicher 2004[4]). The SOS Children's Village organisation requires this information for the development of the organisation but, at the same time, it was putting itself to the test: does SOS Children's Villages act in accordance with the UN Convention on the Rights of the Child – and according to its own guidelines?

How SOS Children's Village adults live today
The value of family and dependable relationships plays a central role in the lives of SOS Children's Village adults today, particularly in Latin America where over 50% of those asked said they spent their free time with their families. On a global level, over two thirds stated that they had a social network on which they could rely and which gave them a sense of security, especially during times of crisis.

Family situation at the time of being asked	
Living in a partnership or married	> 60% (globally)
One or two children	> 50% (globally)

Living situation		
Evaluation of their own standard of housing in comparison to the standard in each country	As equal or better: 72% in El Salvador 47% in South Africa	As lower: 37% in Honduras 23% in Morocco
Content with their own standard of housing		70% (globally)

---

4   The statements reproduced here are only an excerpt from the Tracking Footprints research results.

Because of the very varied cultural circumstances, we were not always able to use the statements about how the SOS Children's Village adults live today directly. For example, in some countries the number of rooms a person lives in does not always say anything about the quality of those rooms. Therefore the global presentation of the results focused on each person's personal evaluation.

Lesson learned

As far as the relevance of the results was concerned, we often found that some results were very meaningful on the level of the country's evaluation, but once these results had been combined with those from other countries they were either totally lost or gave us a "non-committal average".

Education and financial situation

Completed high school or college	50%
Completed an apprenticeship	> 50%
Content with their financial situation	40%

Jobs and education were a high priority in the personal development of SOS Children's Village adults. Many of them had completed a high school or college education, but in general very few of them had completed a university education.

The majority of those questioned had been able to establish themselves on the job market. However, for some people it had been very difficult to stay in one job for a long time. 60 percent of those asked were only just able to manage on what they were earning.

Experiences in SOS Children's Villages

One of the most common reasons why children are admitted to an SOS Children's Village is that they have lost either one or both of their parents. 80 percent of those asked talked about their positive relationships within the SOS Children's Village, especially with their SOS Children's Village mother. Particular emphasis was placed on the support they received in their personal development and in choosing a career. Some people expressed their great thanks - mainly to the SOS Children's Village mother and to the organisation as a whole, which many of them refer to and see as their "family" ("When I entered SOS it changed my life."). This is of high value to many of those questioned.

50 percent of those asked also had a good relationship with the people in their neighbourhood.

On the other hand there were those who saw their experiences in the time they spent in an SOS Children's Village critically. Some mentioned a lack of support in training for a job, ("There was nobody to keep our moral high and to encourage us to pull our socks up to succeed in our education.") as well as inadequate behaviour of the carers. This included psychological and physical abuse.

Many people said that the SOS Children's Village facilities did not adequately cover the great need for support in the transitional phase between adolescence and adulthood. Many reported that contact was broken once they had moved out of the SOS Children's Village facilities. The adults-to-be saw this as a lack of interest on the part of the organisation, as well as a deficiency in the organisation's support and after-care methods.

Learning from the SOS Children's Village adults' experiences

The statements made by those asked – and consequently our research results – show that on the whole SOS Children's Villages played a successful role in helping children and young people to develop positively. However, there were also areas where there is an immense need for change and improvement. The suggestions made by the SOS Children's Village adults are as follows:

Confirmation of SOS Children's Village's efforts	Need for change
Fulfilling the basic needs of the children is taken care of: security, a home, a family, food, clothing, etc.	More attention should be paid to the individual child (love, communication, etc.); stronger support for contact with the biological family; total prevention of physical and psychological abuse
Dependable relationships, in particular with the SOS Children's Villages mother and the SOS Children's Villages brothers and sisters	Try to keep in touch more with SOS Children's Village adults; more stability within the co-worker group; better methods of choosing new employees and the professionalisation of SOS Children's Village co-workers; more support for the co-workers in their work
Availability of good schools and the possibility of doing an apprenticeship	Better and improved support and guidance in the process of becoming independent and earning a living. Better support of integration into society outside the SOS Children's Village

To continue questioning and the long-term effects – contributing to the development of the organisation

In part, research involves thinking along the lines of, "Where will the realisations we have gathered lead us? Where and how can we implement what we have learned?" The answers we received to our research questions were not, in themselves, the final goal of our project. To continue to want to find things out is a part of a living development. The global results from the Tracking Footprints project which we gathered in the first three years have already been used in other projects and in generating further ideas. This is what is known as living knowledge. By constantly questioning its efforts, an organisation such as SOS Children's Villages, is able to increase the possibilities of carrying out far-reaching analysis that will lead to an improvement in its care concept.

The project leadership team was invited to take part in a research seminar in Africa, in order to provide theoretical and practical research expertise. Exchanges such as this one ensure that the possibilities of learning and transferring knowledge within the organisation are used to the full and are put into practice in reality. Giving and taking, dealing openly with the results and trying to understand each other's needs, accepting expertise from the project leadership team - these are all helpful and supportive, as well as undeniable if we want to learn from our targeted knowledge communication and our experiences; i.e. to see learning possibilities and to make the most of them. A process such as this requires trust and mutual respect between all the partners. If this attitude is authentic, it will become an important pillar in building relationships. The transfer of knowledge can develop into a successful flow of natural communication.

Opening up new options for action – using the research results effectively
An organisation can foster competence in its field through the use of application-orientated research.

As far as organisational development is concerned, it can be said that the Tracking Footprints project has been successful so far: we have been able to increase awareness of the necessity of carrying out strategically anchored research through our tangible research activity within the organisation. The next aim would be to integrate the strategy and experiences successfully into the organisation's tasks and to "use what we have learned from this project for our future projects." (Richard Pichler, secretary-general SOS-Kinderdorf International). Knowledge that has been gained from research gives an organisation many possibilities for action and has long-lasting effects.

In a nutshell, socio-ecological communication cannot be achieved with written reports alone. Socio-ecological knowledge increases the options for dealing with matters in the fields of socio-ecology in a particular manner. It influences these options and is, in itself, a part of this field of activity. Communicating this knowledge, especially to non-specialist co-workers, could widen their range of actions and change social practices in the direction of greater sustainability (cf. Schmidt 2003, www.isoe.de). It is exactly this sustainability that should be achieved within the SOS Children's Village organisation by the targeted use of our research results. How can SOS Children's Villages learn from the experiences of the SOS Children's Village

adults in order to improve its care methods? How can this knowledge be blended into the development of the organisation? Those responsible in all the various countries have now been given the task of implementing the knowledge gained from this project into the work plans. This means, for example, that:

- Measures are being taken to increase awareness amongst various levels of co-workers of the relevant topics (for example, the process of becoming independent, social integration, keeping in touch with SOS Children's Village adults, after-care, contact and working with the biological families, the avoidance of violence and abuse, etc.),
- Training courses are being planned for SOS Children's Village co-workers,
- The relevant topics are now being included in training programmes,
- The findings are having an effect on the job profiles for co-workers (SOS Children's Village mothers, youth leaders, village directors, social workers, etc.),
- Improvement of the working conditions of SOS co-workers (help and support in the daily work, psychological counselling, etc.)

The good practice examples from these measures taken should be filtered in order to be able to make them available for everybody in a future, global exchange of knowledge. The process of practical implementation of our results is then to be evaluated as to its level of sustainability so that the recommendations made by those questioned in this study will also have long-term effects.

Taking stock of our experiences

The knowledge we gained from our project should be made available for other organisations. If we take stock of our experiences from the Tracking Footprints project, we can show that we have gained a wealth of experience:

What was beneficial?

- Having the personal commitment and interest of our partners
- Having the support of our superiors and decision-makers
- Having the acceptance of expert knowledge and respecting it
- Having the courage to give former SOS Children's Village children the status of experts
- Having previous knowledge and experience of research in the countries where we operate
- Having existing contacts to universities in these countries
- Having an up-to-date database on the whereabouts of SOS Children's Village adults

What did the project vindicate or prove?

- The participative and appreciative approach of the project management
- Working together with external partners and critical friends
- Dealing carefully with "foreignness" and interculturalism
- Flexibility in relation to making compromises and finding a consensus
- Open communication and analysing the problems of the research results
- Being strict and persistent when presenting scientific principles and standards
- A continued effort to create a link between the SOS Children's Village work and the research activities

What were the obstacles?

- Structural changes taking place within the international management level during the middle of the implementation phase of the project, which meant we had a new group to report to.
- Sometimes the project leadership team had unrealistically high expectations of the participative approach.
- The global demands of the research design: one tool for all countries and cultures.
- The global demands in assimilating the data: "The global consolidation of data may be very desirable, but at the end of the day, it does not make sense. The great danger is that the results then become an "average" of everything. In my opinion, it would make more sense to work on a regional or continental basis in order to see the trends more clearly, and then to project them onto a global level. Then we could ask whether these trends are also relevant for other regions and continents." (Richard Pichler, secretary-general SOS-Kinderdorf International).
- During the creation stage of this project, research was still being seen as a "new fashion" within SOS Children's Villages. It had no strategic fixed point at the time.
- The project leadership team had very little opportunity to get close to the practical SOS Children's Village work in the field to experience the different cultural starting points.

How would we do it differently today?

- We would think about how to use the results right from the start and would integrate this into the design-development.
- Communication with the decision-makers: "Even if it means the project takes longer, it is necessary to bring in the decision makers who are going to be affected in order to get their approval for the concept." (Richard Pichler, secretary-general SOS-Kinderdorf International).
- We would check the decision-makers' expectations of the project more often.

- As part of the concept, we would strongly fix the need for all project steering partners to meet in person.
- We would create a livelier network of project partners and ensure that they communicate more amongst themselves.
- We would remove the global demands and replace them with more room for manoeuvre for country-specific aims and challenges.
- We would include the target group of the research project (the SOS Children's Village adults) in the concept development stage.
- We would include PR and marketing activities for the project as one of the central requirements right from the start.

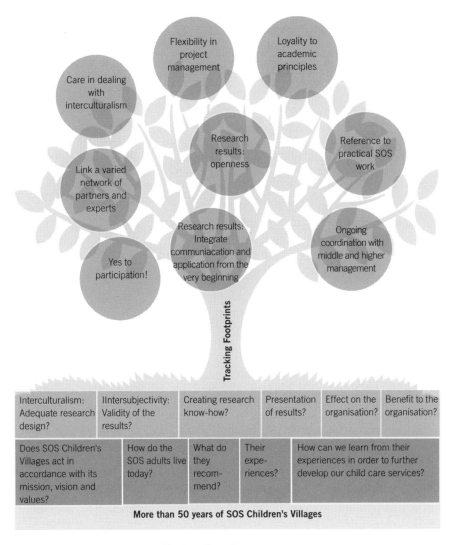

Figure 5   Lessons learned – Tracking Footprints

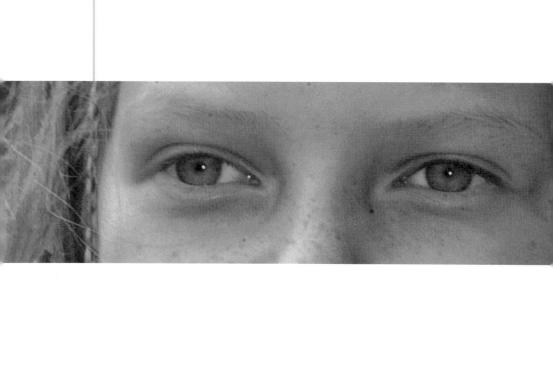

Gerhild Rafetseder

Harvesting

Gathering experiences for dreams of the future

Somewhere in the tide of events we completed the valuation interview process. During this process – I keep having to think about it – we formed pairs. We had the help of a questionnaire and spent hours with each other trying to find out about the other person – not too deeply, but deeply enough to find out why we both work for SOS Children's Villages. Sometimes the process turned into a heart-rending voyage into the past. A few times I had to catch my breath and sometimes even had to try hard not to cry out loud. When I suddenly thought about my family and our beautiful farm my feelings and emotions were so strong ...

Ian Kluckow, Zimbabwe, October 2002

What happens when you manage to bring movement into the wealth of experience that the co-workers of an international organisation have? What forces are set free? People become infected by the buzz and new dimensions are created!

Harvesting is not only a tool for the transfer of knowledge – it is far more than that: it was designed as a human resource and organisational development project which revolved around formal and informal exchanges between co-workers.

The following article describes the planning and implementation of a process for long-standing co-workers, giving them a chance to exchange and generate experiences from a very personal point of view.

The management's aim was to collect the experiences of what made SOS Children's Villages what it is today – before these experiences became forgotten in the annals of history – and to pass this information on to both more recent and future co-workers. This happened in the context of a period of restructuring within the organisation and after 50 successful years of organisational history.

Those who have been working in the projects for years and sometimes even decades and have thus formed part of the history of the organisation were given the chance to talk about their experiences on a personal level and were able to bring in their knowledge, just like bringing in the harvest. It was a project of mammoth dimensions! Three Harvesting seminars were held. They comprised 600 years of experience from over 50 years of SOS Children's Village work, and included 52 co-workers from four continents, 43 countries and speaking 27 different native languages. Making this incredible amount of organisational history visible led to the project taking on its own energy that went much further than merely collecting memories and making sure that existing knowledge did not get lost.

The organisation profited from an impressive "harvest" in terms of stories about experiences that could now be made available to all co-workers, from the motivational factor this gave to all the participants and from a wealth of innovative ideas and individual projects.

The quotations we have used here originated either from the anonymous documents arising from the workshops or from the feedback questionnaires. Some of the original quotations have been translated from Spanish or French.

The task

The co-workers of an organisation that has given thousands of children a family and a future over the decades are a motley crew. Some of them carried out pioneering work at the start; others have survived wars or the consequences of natural disasters. All of them have done this with an incredible amount of personal commitment and have, therefore, gained a lot of special expertise.

The organisation's top management declared that this project would be an integral part of their international human resources development and established the following aims:

- For the exchange of experiences to focus on the preservation of values and educational topics between co-workers in leading positions, who have been with the organisation for at least ten years.
- To develop a strategy for communicating this knowledge (and wisdom) from long-standing co-workers (for example, via the SOS Intranet – an internal Internet platform that can be accessed by co-workers worldwide).
- To increase the motivation of long-standing co-workers in respect of new strategic developments within the SOS Children's Villages organisation.

A two-week programme had to be worked out and offered in the form of workshops known in English as "Harvesting", in French as "La Moisson" and in Spanish as "Cosecha".

Planning

The planning of the Harvesting programme was carried out together with the decision-makers at a continental level. The guiding topics – and for most of the countries participating, current topics – were suggested by the management at local level.

The workshops

We held three workshops over a period of three years. The participants came from various cultural and linguistic backgrounds and professions and were mainly from middle management. This brought about a huge diversity within the groups.

- Harvesting: the first workshop was for English-speaking co-workers and was held in Innsbruck, Austria, in October 2002. There were 20 participants from 16 countries, spanning three continents: Europe, Africa and Asia.
- Cosecha: One year later, 20 Spanish-speaking co-workers from Europe and Latin-America met in Innsbruck, Austria.
- La Moisson: fifteen co-workers from ten African, European and Asian countries met in Morocco in April 2004 for a French-language workshop.

Programme concept

The local management briefed their co-workers on the expectations of the programmes. The team organising the workshops answered any questions and cleared up any misconceptions before the workshops started by speaking to the participants on the phone.

The greatest challenge in organising the programme and estimating the times for each day and each part of the workshop lay in the (expected) cultural differences between the participants as well as the language barrier. "Keep it simple" gained a special meaning when using any specialist vocabulary. It was very useful during the planning stage that the team organising the event had already gained plenty of experience from organising earlier events involving international groups.

We made sure that the workshop programme was not packed full to the last minute, allowing spare time for unexpected developments. We wanted to avoid structuring the programme too strictly, thus allowing us either to cut parts out, to move them around or to leave them open.

Main topics

We drew on topics which were the current focus of attention in each of the participating regions and countries to define the main themes of the workshops:

- Mission and the strategic development of SOS Children's Villages: at this time the SOS Children's Village organisation was setting its strategic initiatives for the next five years and re-organising the continental management level. This had a direct effect on the management levels immediately below this and caused some co-workers to become unsure of their own roles and responsibilities within the new structure. Therefore, this topic was deliberately selected as an item for debate.
- Prevention of child abandonment - strengthening the family: the organisation had opened up to carry out preventative work with families world-wide, and in view of social and political developments this was a high priority topic. The framework for this topic was to organise an intensive exchange on programmes that had already been implemented and to see how they could possibly be included in new projects.
- Leadership – to lead and be led within the framework of the organisation and in the context of different cultures: the participants all came

from the middle-management level, which meant they were very interested in dealing with this topic

Choosing a method – Appreciative Inquiry (AI)

We decided to use Appreciative Inquiry as the method best suited both to the job we wanted to do and to the organisation's culture. Appreciative Inquiry concentrates on finding out ways to effect changes and solutions for dealing with them. The definitive theme is to find methods that already work and to make more use of them. People are made aware of what the reality should be, because an organisation will move in the direction in which its members guide it (cf. Maleh 2001, p. 32).

Appreciative Inquiry was used as the framework for the programme. This method comes from the field of organisational development and was created in the 1980s. The heart of this method is to track down the positive potential within an organisation or a system through the members or the people acting within the system, in order to use these methods as a basis for future projects. The difference between this method and Good Practice Sharing is that the storyteller in the latter is not always identical with the person successfully carrying out the tasks described in the story. AI concentrates on the personal contribution of each of the individual participants which can lead to a transformation within a system. The main purpose is for the participants to discover their own life-giving-forces, such as the values they hold, their pattern of relationships and their personal strengths, and to see how these forces can bring about a successfully completed task.

This type of discovery and the valuation that goes along with it was a new experience for the seminar's participants. The storyteller was able to create his or her "own" reality through sharing his or her own stories with others. The storytellers were able to see their inner strengths in relationship to other experiences and also to see their potential. They were able to analyse their own actions and to see themselves as experts in the field. This was achieved by telling stories and working on these stories in groups. By aligning what one person had experienced with the experiences of another and the organisational culture, positive strengths were filtered out that could then be used highly motivationally in future projects.

Common rules and rituals were created through constant exchange with others. Each participant's own view of the world was constantly put to the test and sometimes critically questioned. Language codes were developed and tried out in order to achieve a level of orientation. Bridges were built to cross the cultural divides. They allowed the participants to gain a deep insight into values and ways of dealing with matters in other parts of the world. For example, one co-worker from Africa approached the seminar leader and explained that she had no idea what her partner was really trying to tell her. She could not understand why her colleague from an eastern European country found the story of a group of brothers and sisters whose parents were alcoholics so special. She said that in her culture, the destructive effects of alcoholism were just not as common as perhaps they were in her discussion partner's country. They finally caught on when the two of them were asked to talk about the definition of alcoholism and about alcoholism as a social problem as well as about the political situation in each of their countries.

As soon as the storyteller's greatest achievement became clear, both of them were able to continue with their discussion.

Table 1 shows how the structure of AI works. The following chapters will deal with more detailed explanations of how it worked with Harvesting.

Phase	Aim	Method	Contents
Phase 1 **Discovery**	Discover your own potential	Appreciative Inquiry	What am I an expert in? Is it interesting for others?
Phase 2 **Dream**	Dream of the future	Imaginative journey	What do I imagine would be a perfect situation in ten years' time? What do I dream about? What has changed? Awakening of enthusiasm for change.
Phase 3 **Design**	Build the future	Symbol	Where do I/we want to go?
Phase 4 **Destiny**	Planning	Plan of action	How can I turn my dreams into reality?

Table 1   The four phases of Appreciative Inquiry

Bringing movement into knowledge

Before we can bring movement into knowledge, we first of all need to establish a good basis for communication between the participants. One of the problems we had was that the language spoken at the workshops was not always everybody's mother tongue. The participants made great efforts to help each other to understand everything. It took a lot of patience and there were some funny moments that arose through linguistic misunderstandings.

Building trust

First of all it was necessary to build trust between the participants in order for our workshops to be constructive: it cannot be taken for granted that people who have never met before will immediately be able to be trusting towards each other. It is imperative to have a warm-up phase when people from different levels of management come together. Within the SOS Children's Villages hierarchy the national directors are above the village directors for example. This meant that both groups found it quite difficult to see the others as equals in terms of leadership.

Political, religious and cultural differences were further challenges that were already being addressed in the warm-up phase by making them apparent in various exercises. The Israeli and Palestinian participants talked about their mutual lack of computer skills. On the first day they realised that they both knew very little about working with computers and that the best thing would be to see if they could not improve their skills by working together.

Choosing an SOS Children's Village facility for all of the workshops certainly helped in building trust amongst the participants and ensuring that they felt happy there.

The participants presented themselves and their work on pin boards to which they stuck brochures, photos, various publications, handcrafted objects and many other items.

Harvesting is not a passive training course, nor is it a workshop with input and speakers. The participants are encouraged to reveal their innermost thoughts and to find out how they have managed to accomplish special achievements.

That is why this introductory phase is so extremely important. Because the trust-building element of AI continues throughout the first three phases, it is necessary to ensure that there are no major distractions or interruptions during this period.

> *"The merit of Harvesting was to give us the time to take a break from our busy lives and to think about where we're going and how we'll get there."*
>
> Ian Kluckow, Zimbabwe, October 2002

| Phase 1: Discovery

> We need to discover how each individual grows when faced with challenges. We also need to learn about the clever strategies that are applied in a system. The foundation of Appreciative Inquiry is how we ourselves assess the events that have led to a change. The building blocks are the strengths, strategies and emotions that can be transposed onto new or different situations.

One of the important tools used during Harvesting is that of telling each other stories, listening to each other's stories and asking questions about them.

SOS Children's Villages can look back on years of traditionally passing on knowledge and educational experience through the telling of stories. These include stories about how the organisation was started, how the idea spread, the first attempts at marketing the organisation, the wonderful success stories from children from all over the world, how terrible catastrophes were faced up to, and so on. These stories have been told all over the world. Thus myths are created within the organisation and express what SOS Children's Villages stands for and what the nature of the organisation is.

Telling stories is an ideal way for an international organisation to spread knowledge as these stories allow the tellers to explain clearly and precisely the contexts in which and the cultural idiosyncracies against which the success was achieved. If co-workers are to be put in the position

of experts – not from the point of view of their role in the organisation, but rather from the point of view of their personalities - then telling stories allows them to show feelings and to reflect much better than any questionnaire would do.

During the first phase of Appreciative Inquiry the co-workers tell stories in order to discover the wealth of knowledge, wisdom and experience they already have.

Method	Aim	Contents
Part 1 **Interviews in pairs**	Telling each other success stories about one of the main topics.	Personal questions to start the Storytelling; two stories about one of the main topics; intensive questioning leads to extracting the root of the stories
Part 2 **Small groups**	To exchange thoughts about all the stories in the small group.	The listener retells the story; everybody formulates the "life-giving-forces" in all the stories.
Part 3 **Plenary**	Presentation	To create a new story about a main topic from all the existing stories.

Table 2   Overview of phase 1 – Discovery

Two participants, who either do not know each other at all, or at least not very well, interview each other in the first part of the discovery phase. They spend a whole morning talking together and telling each other about the experience from their field of work that has impressed them most and where they played an active role.

What is important here is the teller's point of reference to the story he or she is telling. Therefore they have to tell a story about themselves rather than about "something". They are encouraged to talk about their actions, their motivations in their actions, their intuition, their feelings and their subjective assessment of the situation. The listener supports this process by actively listening and asking questions. When both partners feel that they have had enough and that the whole picture has been painted, they try to analyse and formulate the strengths that lie behind each action.

> *"I felt that the pair work – the Storytelling – was very moving. It's quite a different thing, whether I read something or if I listen to a story that my partner is telling me. You get far more than just the story. There are the fears and the joy. It wasn't just words I was listening to. The emotional level was much stronger. I could feel the reality of it all. It was a huge enrichment."*
>
> Celia Etchegarray, Paraguay, 2005

The questioning was started by asking leading questions about the partner's personal background and career. Particular points of interest were questions about why the person had decided to work for SOS Children's Villages, how he or she had experienced his or her early days with the organisation and how he or she saw the organisation today with all its strengths and weaknesses.

> *"After crossing the city that was lying in ruins, where everything had been stolen, (even the underground cables had been taken so that people could sell the copper wire), it was like a vision when I discovered the SOS Children's Village, where everyone was leading a normal life. The children were playing, the co-workers were going about their jobs, there was a green field and flowers (...) the feeling of peace and safety allowed me to sense the inner strength of an organisation, whose culture and commitment is to create a safe haven for children, where the injured and sick can be healed without having to worry about bureaucracy and the laws."*
>
> Anonymous Harvesting participant

> *"I seriously admire SOS Children's Villages' contribution to humanity in general, and in particular what it does for children in need. It is such a simple and practical philosophy – SOS mother, brothers and sisters, family and the (village) community."*
>
> Anonymous Harvesting participant

The next sequence of questions included a central question about one of the three main topics of the workshop (mission; prevention of child abandonment: strengthening the family; leadership; cf. p. 122).

Extract from the guidelines: the sequence of questions on the topic of prevention

"I would like you to think about those experiences you have had with families who were in danger of abandoning their children and to tell me about any lasting impressions that you had!"

Allow time for the story to be told
- Why was this experience so meaningful for you?
- What was your contribution?
- How did SOS Children's Villages support you?
- What kind of support from other persons or from outside was important?
- In your opinion, what was the most important factor contributing to the success?
- How were the values of courage, responsibility, trust and reliability experienced here?

The result of the interviews in pairs can be a short form of the story where particular emphasis is placed on the core elements, or even just on one comment that hits the nail on the head.

> *"There was this woman who wanted to kill her two children and commit suicide. Her husband had chased her away. She couldn't find a job or anywhere to live. She could see no way out. That day she met a friend on the street and that friend brought her to me. She was desperate and crying as she told me her tragic story. She was able to leave her children with us in the SOS Social Centre while she went to work. We were able to find her an apprenticeship as a hairdresser. She also attended evening classes on personality development. After many arguments, she finally left her violent husband. She took trouble with her appearance and became much more self-confident. Her children were good at school. Today she's working as a volunteer in our social centre and is on the way to fulfilling her dream of opening her own hairdressing salon."*
>
> Dalia Souza, Venezuela 2003

During the second part of "Discovery", three or four interview pairs join together to form small groups in order to exchange ideas amongst themselves. The listener has to retell the others' stories. These stories are then analysed in the small groups and a joint decision is made as to what is to be presented to the whole group. That can either be one particular story that, in the view of all the participants, underlines the main topic best, or it can be parts of several stories that have recurred or highlights and deep emotions that the participants filter out in order to create a new story. The participants take quotations and parts of the existing stories and put them together so that the new stories contain all the elements that were typical of the original stories. These are then presented to the whole group so that the extracts or "jewels" from all the stories are made available to everybody.

"What was so incredible about this exercise was that, even though we all came from different cultures and play different roles within the organisation, we all see the same challenges, use the same sources of strength and spread the same message."

Margret Nkrumah, Ghana, 2003

"SOS Children's Villages is based on a wonderful idea that is embedded in a great concept. Having your good work appreciated spurs on your personal growth and you feel fulfilled in your work. The organisation spreads love, trust and security and makes it easy for its co-workers to live their beliefs. The basis of leadership is creativity, planning and implementation that are influenced by understanding and honesty. The co-workers are responsible for the children and young people and are able to hone their professional talents. The key factors are teamwork and commitment. That is why our work is of such a high quality. Internal and external clarity are important. Working for SOS Children's Villages is more like a way of behaving, a philosophy rather than merely a job."

Anonymous Harvesting participant

Phase 2: Dream

Visualising dreams becomes an organisational development tool. The participants imagine an ideal situation in the context of one of the main topics and in the conditions in which they are working. Most of these dreams stem from personal experience.

Sharing dreams is only possible once trust has been established. This phase can be very difficult to implement if the participants come from an organisational culture where competition is very strong. Co-workers who see their organisational culture as being very paternalistic and are not used to talking

about their own ideas and efforts can find it very difficult to break down these barriers. Therefore, in order to avoid any possible dilemmas, we had the participants talk about their dreams about their work location and the organisation itself rather than about where they saw themselves career-wise in the future.

Method	Aim	Contents
Part 1 **Dream Voyage**	Inner concentration	Vision of the future: what has changed?
Part 2 **Working alone**	Personal comments on the manifestation of the vision.	Writing down ideas.
Small groups	To increase the pool of ideas. To create courage and motivation.	Sharing thoughts and visions.
Part 3 **Plenary**	The collective message for the future is presented as imaginatively as possible.	Presentation

Table 3   Overview of phase 2 – Dream

The dream phase starts with a dream voyage. In many articles, this phase is seen as the most tricky and sensitive as the participants have to bare their souls. However, having just completed the first phase of discovery where their self-confidence has been increased they are then able to express their desires and dreams in regard to their working conditions.

An example of a dream voyage (abridged)

The room is darkened; quiet music is playing in the background. A PowerPoint presentation is showing pictures of harvests. The journey starts quietly with many pauses between the instructions: "You open your eyes. It is the year 2014. You have just completed a long journey in time. You shake yourself awake and look around. You are at work - in your office or in the SOS Children's Village. You go for a walk. Everywhere you see happy, laughing children. They take no notice of you because they are so wrapped up in their games and activities. Your co-workers are working with great concentration. They seem relaxed and happy. You realise that a lot has happened whilst you were asleep. What has changed?"

After a period of time that depends on the needs of the participants, everyone is brought back to the present. The participants describe what they think has changed; what they have contributed to these changes and what kind of support they have received. Anybody who feels like it can capture their dream by drawing it:

"I drew a can of Coke because my dream is that one day SOS Children's Villages will be as famous as this brand and we will be within reach of every child. At the same time my deepest wish is that SOS Children's Villages will not be needed at all anymore."

Mario Brousa, Ethiopia 2002

"I will only dream of good things and most of all, I'll believe in them. Sometimes I have to pause, or even venture into the darkness. I have to get help and support. I have to be thankful for those people who protect me from having my dreams interrupted."

Alassan Gomina, Benin, 2004

In the next step, everybody's dreams are shared amongst small groups. The instructions are explicitly to listen, accept and not to judge. The aim here is not to make judgments, but rather to talk about the dreams, exchange thoughts and thus achieve the first step towards putting the visions into concrete terms.

"In order for my dreams and visions to be fulfilled, I need other peoples' dreams too. I can see that it isn't the differences between us that are important. What counts are the similarities."

Francis Santos, Philippines, 2002

The groups then prepared a presentation. They were told to make them as original as possible and to play with all the senses. They wrote poems, composed songs, performed sketches and built dream-ships. Their imagination seemed to have no end:

"We have chartered a big ship and are sailing to Africa along the west coast, where we call in at every country. There have been big announcements before we get there and anybody who is interested can either come with us for part of the journey or just come aboard for a while. It will be the biggest ever fund-raising project for West Africa."

Daniel Dejean, Austria 2004

Phase 3 Design

The potential from the dream phase is to be developed during the design phase. A bridge is built from the past to the future where the positive energy that was gained from a past success is combined with the dream of the future to achieve new forms of action.

The third phase deals with turning the potential of the dreams into innovative ideas that can be implemented. The participants' experiences from the discovery phase help assess fears for the future, tangible barriers and doubts and to turn them into positive energies. The participants help and encourage each other to think about taking concrete steps as well as to think about the partners or alliances they might need.

Method	Aim	Content
Individual work	Symbol	The participants return to their own strengths and dreams by carrying out a meditative, creative activity (e.g. kneading beeswax).

Table 4   Overview of phase 3 – Design

Working (kneading) with coloured beeswax helps the participants to think about the near future. This is hard work for the hands and helps to free their heads so that ideas that might previously have gone to sleep are suddenly awakened and the support from the group means that the dreams come closer once more. The aim of this phase is to design a construction plan and to think about how best to realise this plan.

Many of the participants experienced this phase as especially meaningful and as pointing the way ahead. On the one hand, the dreams were still lingering and on the other, the real hurdles were also still visible.

"It is possible to have a bridge into the future; a bridge that is strong enough to walk on. But it's difficult to think in the future. I don't know what path the organisation's going to take in the future or whether my dream – especially my understanding of the leadership – will fit in. But that's also a source of strength for me: what is really exciting is that we all have the same dream; that there are so many people who are committed to this dream and who believe in the aims and values of our organisation."

Daniel Miranda, Uruguay, 2005

The participants also considered their surroundings, "Where do I need support?", "What have been the hurdles that should no longer be there?" "What is the most important thing I need in order to be able to make a start?" Many of them began to think about active forms of co-operation, possible support and the necessary resources required.

"We were all amazed when we discovered that all our dreams already have a foundation in reality. That makes them attainable visions."

Anonymous Harvesting participant

The participants then created a symbol from these thoughts. These symbols were to show strength and determination as well as personal commitment. The colours here were just as important as the shapes, and in many cases the participants also created a synonym for their mottos.

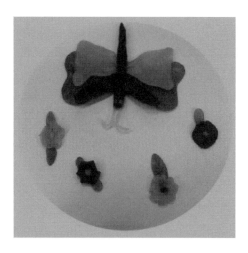

Vision Design

"The symbol is a colourful butterfly. Green is for hope and the desire that our dreams will come true. Yellow is the light, the knowledge that illuminates our path. Blue is the SOS Children's Villages organisation as it awakens and supports the mothers and the community who, at the same time, are in the process of discovering themselves or developing and organising themselves. The flowers represent well-trained co-workers who are able to meet the needs of our children, who support and defend the rights of the children and the community."

Dalia Souza, Venezuela 2004

Phase 4: Destiny

By creating plans of action with goals for each stage, the participants are able to turn their visions into projects that can be realised and thereby influence the future. Their continued path in their day-to-day work can be influenced by defining the steps to turn new ideas into reality.

Following the phase of working alone and designing the future, the participants next have to design a plan of action for a project. This brings events full circle: the success factors from the stories that have been told are combined with the dreams of the future in order to be used in a real project.

Method	Aim	Content
Part 1 **Working alone**	Plan of action	The project that has just been imagined is brought into a framework that can be realised.
Part 2 **Working alone**	Milestones	Important stage goals are set and described in detail.
Part 3 **Plenary**	Walking down the path	In order to internalise the milestones, the participants walk along their path and share their experiences with the others.

Table 5   Overview of phase 4 – Destiny

The participants wrote down the concrete steps including a time frame and the resources required. Because the participants knew that one month after the workshop they had to report on it in two further evaluation steps, they found this phase very intensive.

In order to internalise their projects the participants "walked" along their milestones showing the short-term aims. They created their paths using a ball of wool and walked to their symbols. Everyone walked along their own paths and spoke aloud about their plans.

The path to the future

The participants have to prepare the way to reach their working goals themselves. They have to hold any necessary discussions with their superiors as well as inform their teams and close colleagues.

This exercise can be best understood when looking at a project that has already been realised: the participant chose a coloured ball of wool, laid out her personal milestones (steps) along the path by using coloured cards (stage goals) and described each individual step including the timeframe, needs and aims. The following text came from the final evaluation, which was sent in one year after the workshop took place:

> *"My project was about the organisation being recognised by national governments. The first milestone: holding two workshops with representatives from the national child-protection agency, youth welfare association and social welfare.*

The second milestone: taking part in a working group to create national standards for accommodating children who cannot grow up with their biological families. Third milestone: to present the document, "Prevention of Child Abandonment: Strengthening the Family", to the authorities at the same time that we ask for recognition, so that they can see that we offer a good alternative and that we are operating within the government guidelines on caring for children."

Anelia Rogelova, Bulgaria, 2003

Writing a diary – Documenting the process

The participants themselves were partly responsible for documenting the process: often – especially in the Storytelling phase – they took hand-written notes and later copied these notes into the computer.

The documentation was supported by photographs and videos. The organisational team collected all the memos and minutes and filed them. They described the events of the workshop and clearly noted any deviations from the plan, any difficult situations and particularly successful sessions. These minutes could then be used to improve the Harvesting processes for future workshops.

The documentation had to be very exact as it was necessary to write reports (in three languages) from them later on. So that the participants also had a voice, quotations were also reproduced word for word.

The project team filed all the materials so that anybody who is interested can have a look whenever they want. All the reports, pictures and daily minutes were put at the disposal of the organisation in the SOS Intranet.

Sustainability: Evaluating the feedback

There were three feedback loops in which the potential of Harvesting was analysed in depth. The results were made available to the management and all co-workers in the SOS Intranet.

Timeframe	Method	Contents
4 weeks after Harvesting	Questionnaire	Concerns the workshop and returning to work afterwards. The participants describe the first steps they have taken to realise their plans and goals.
6 months after Harvesting	Questionnaire	Concerns the implementation and the continuation of the projects.
12 months after Harvesting	Short report	A short report about the process and status of the project.

Table 6   Timeframe – Evaluation

The following charts show the replies we received concerning the results of all the evaluations[1] (Harvesting 2002, 2003, 2004). We analysed everything on three levels – personal and individual, team and organisational – and took into account how they corresponded to the fields of knowledge transfer, motivation and human resource/organisational development.

Levels	Background and replies
Personal and individual level	Use and effects on the participants personally. They mainly recorded that they had felt a change in their behaviour towards a more positive outlook and promotion.
Team level	The participants noted a change in their immediate field of work. They felt there was an improved use of existing management tools (performance appraisal, delegation of responsibilities). The inclusion of children and young people from the SOS Children's Village facilities was also mentioned in this part.
Organisation/ the entire organisation	This section included the extended field of work of the participants. Much mention was made of including the board of directors more. Furthermore, Harvesting was talked about in a wide field and used as a concept for training and development possibilities.

Table 7   Overview of the levels

---

1   Total number of replies n = 213; we took any statements that were repeated into consideration, attributed them and included them.

Items	Replies
Transfer of knowledge	Concerned how to transfer knowledge: the stories that were used, the workshop methods and processes and the exchange of documents.
Motivation	Comments on the topics of gaining strength and new courage, a feeling of belonging to the organisation and the realisation of dreams.
Human resource and organisational development	Included all the changes that the participants noticed in their surroundings following Harvesting. These were aspects such as new training methods as well as restructuring to increase efficiency and the promotion of Harvesting participants.

Table 8   Overview of the items

The first diagram shows the number of replies we received for each level. The participants saw their participation in Harvesting as a definite motivational factor on the personal and individual level. At a team and organisation level, the participants clearly saw the topics regarding knowledge transfer as the main goal. What was interesting here for the participants was using the didactic methods and management tools they learned in the context of their daily tasks. Very many co-workers reported that they were able to use Appreciative Inquiry in workshops or as parts of seminars, or even just in the SOS Children's Village itself. They were able to use the dream and design phases in close connection within the local cultural contexts. The effectiveness of this method is intensified by the use of rituals and symbols with which the local people are familiar.

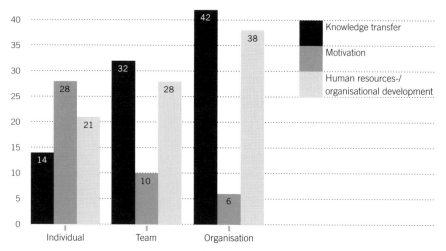

Diagram 1   The number of replies per level (n=219)

The following diagrams show a more exact breakdown of the results. We used original quotations and abridged reports to give the charts a qualitative dimension.

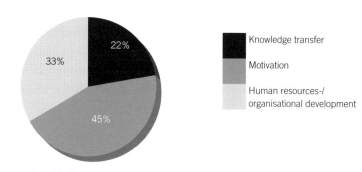

Diagram 2   Personal and Individual level (n=63)

More than half the replies from the participants regarding the personal and individual level said they experienced highly increased motivation. They saw their participation as a milestone.

Being able to exchange ideas and information on an international basis and being able to find a new personal relationship with the organisation as a whole

were important factors for them. They saw being permitted to take part in the workshop as a great honour and it gave them many positive impulses for their work in the future. Furthermore, they mentioned that they felt they had developed personally through the appreciative attitude that lies behind the method of Appreciative Inquiry. In their replies regarding knowledge transfer the participants clearly referred to benefits on a personal level as they had been able to share knowledge with their colleagues and saw this as "making new friends". In the project section there was a wide range of sometimes very personal matters listed such as some things they had been putting off doing for a long time, including decisions to make in their own families, taking courses, time-planning and planning their lives.

> "Appreciation of the path I have already trodden within the organisation. I have rediscovered memories that I thought I had lost."
>
> Daniel Miranda, Uruguay, 2005

Sometime the participants' attitude towards themselves, their co-workers and their own culture had changed:

> "Because we don't appreciate our own countries and because of our selfish desire to get as far away from Africa as possible, we are unable to see our own value. Last October in Innsbruck, I was introduced to a different way of looking at things. It was a very simple but new concept to me: when you want to change something for the better or build something, begin by looking at the things you got right rather than at the things you did wrong."
>
> Margret Nkrumah, Ghana, 2003

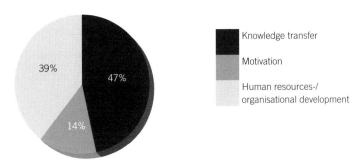

■ Knowledge transfer

■ Motivation

☐ Human resources-/ organisational development

Diagram 3   Team level (n=70)

The *team level* was particularly affected by the transfer of new knowledge and the communication of experiences to all the working fields by those in management positions after they took part in Harvesting. They were able to use the methods they had learned to achieve more intensive exchanges and to try out proven specialist knowledge from other countries and adapt it to their own needs. Projects which benefited on this level were, for example, the mothers' meetings, which were restructured, and changes were made to performance appraisals.

"When I've been implementing what I learned in my daily work, I've had to re-define relationships. This is particularly true in the day-to-day tasks with the SOS mothers and co-workers. I have left much more time for listening to the experiences my co-workers have had and this has definitely strengthened the commitment towards the work being done in the SOS Children's Village."

Anonymous Harvesting participant

"Since I attended Harvesting I now bring back some of the youths that are already living independent lives into the village. They sit down with the children and then they start to tell stories. They tell about how they came to the village and about their dreams for the future. The little ones learn how to deal with their fears from the bigger ones. They have all had similar fates and that helps everybody. I think we've had fewer problems since we've been doing this."

Ratnadurai Divakar, Sri Lanka, 2003

The planning tools have improved the decision-making skills of the co-workers and have helped them to integrate their projects into the surrounding neighbourhood.

"Each of my co-workers bases his plan of action on the yearly plan for the project. During the planning phase we do exactly the same as we did at Harvesting: discovery, dream, building bridges and accurate planning."

Anonymous Harvesting participant

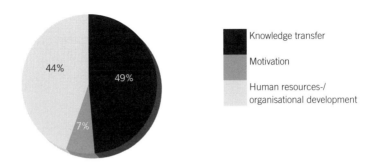

44%

49%

7%

Knowledge transfer

Motivation

Human resources-/
organisational development

Diagram 4   Organisation/the entire organisation level (n=86)

Very often the participants mentioned that they now had more opportunities for exchanging information with various board members with whom they had previously had little contact, for example, the boards of the national associations. The diagram also shows that the Harvesting participants had been promoted, which had an effect on the organisational level. This, as opposed to the team level, was usually at least at national level, but often also on a continental or world-wide level. Furthermore, the participants described the increased use of networks for the whole organisation (for example, the Internet platform, regular exchanges of documents and giving each other feedback).

One thing that was made very clear was that, when taking the step from the virtual project to actual measures within the organisation, the co-workers often had to confront friction and limitations within their local circumstances.

> *"Sometimes my aims clash with those of the current national annual plan. Anything extra in the way of plans of action has to be budgeted for. This is difficult as we are always talking about cutbacks and saving money."*
>
> Anonymous Harvesting participant

If changes are to be made within the organisation, it is necessary to receive the agreement of the next level of management, whether this is the immediate boss or the board of directors. This is a decisive moment as it will prove how much positive energy the participant has taken with him or her from the workshop to help him or her surmount the hurdles.

"I am constantly explaining to our board of directors that we have to see things in a positive light. Many are interested; others still need time. I would like to be able to work closely together with them and see that I can bring about some changes."

Margaret Nkrumah, Ghana, 2002

Is Harvesting a knowledge transfer tool?

What happens when we manage to bring movement into the wealth of experience of the co-workers in an international organisation? I mentioned the answer to this at the beginning of my article: people become infected by the buzz and new dimensions are created. The programme made it possible to make the exchange of knowledge a useful tool specifically for organisational development. How was that possible?

The knowledge management strategies we used were based on principles from the field of qualitative social research. Harvesting particularly reflected the aspect that knowledge is generated through an intense analysis of social realities.

The trick of Harvesting is that it tracks down the co-workers' implicit knowledge and makes it explicit. It turns it from unarticulated knowledge that is dependent on experience into articulated knowledge that is independent of the person who generated it. It is not only the co-worker's factual knowledge that is important for an organisation but also their intuitive ability to act appropriately. SOS Children's Villages is aware as an organisation that it is only their co-workers' actual knowledge that makes sense and can be used to overcome problems.

It is essential for an organisation to place great value on the knowledge and experience of its co-workers and project groups. Every single process within the organisation is dependent on the people in the organisation and without their knowledge, ability and good will all these processes will come to nothing. The existing knowledge has to be made apparent and must be exchanged. If knowledge does not flow within an organisation the result is that co-workers have a constant uphill struggle, the wheel has to be continually re-invented and it can even lead to a total breakdown.

It is especially important when dealing with technical systems for supporting communication – these are aspects such as rules, norms and complex, formal organisational structures as well as paths of communication in our day-to-day work – that these aspects are made clear and simple. It is possible to exchange concepts via technical systems; however it is not possible to exchange the intuitive ability to act appropriately in a given situation in the same way.

In a highly complex organisation the exchange of knowledge is becoming increasingly important as a single strategy towards improving co-worker skills. The co-workers have to be able to filter the information that is relevant to their daily tasks from the flood of information they receive. They have to be able to talk about it amongst themselves, pass on their knowledge to others, continually learn new things and be able to put these into effect in their day-to-day work as efficiently as possible (cf. Reinmann-Rothmeier et al. 2001, p. 22).

The burst of innovation which collecting and sharing knowledge can create is quite amazing. If an organisation takes development programmes such as Harvesting seriously as a part of their knowledge management programme, then this will eventually lead to implementation of the desired changes.

Tips, tricks and experiences

The organisational team had plenty of time in between the three workshops to think about the methods and to improve on them. There were a number of aspects where it became clear that there was scope for improvement in future workshops:

Daily minutes
The process of the workshops was documented from the first day onwards and the organisational team was able to evaluate these minutes. The strengths and weaknesses of the moderation and the group's energy were reflected in quick-fire answer sessions. Any changes, disruptions or successes were noted in the daily minutes. Team meetings were held to discuss these documents and they helped to make any necessary changes to the programme. It was

possible to improve the processes of each workshop as far as clarity and structure were concerned.

Methods that can irritate

As the participants were all either managers or people in leading positions, they were expecting a rational and structured programme. Therefore, the methods we used in the workshop led to some initial irritation. Most of the participants were used to attending training workshops that were on a lecture basis. We gave the participants a lot of chances to voice their opinions in quick-fire question-and-answer sessions and gave them plenty of time to think about the methods. We found that this led to a more positive attitude towards the methods used.

Main topics

We found that having the main topics as an elemental basis for the whole of the workshops meant that the participants found it easier to see the relationship between the theory and what they needed in their day-to-day work.

The first topic was "Mission and the strategic development of SOS Children's Villages". This dealt with the core idea of the organisational culture. We found that, especially during the restructuring phase of the organisation, this topic made a lot of sense, particularly for the participants who had been with the organisation for many years.

The second topic was "Prevention of child abandonment: Strengthening the family". This is one of the organisation's eight strategic initiatives. It was chosen because it needed to be implemented as soon as possible. As this topic was so pragmatic, it meant that a lot of concrete initiatives and innovative thoughts were constructed here to develop this strategy in the future.

The third topic was "Leading and being led". This dealt with parts of co-worker development. It became apparent that many of the participants had formally experienced the power structures within the organisation when they discussed this topic. Some taboos were also mentioned. These were then clarified and we were able to deal with them too.

A heterogeneous group

There were incredible differences amongst the participants as regards culture, linguistic abilities and, in particular, their hierarchical placement

within the organisation. We had to build up mutual trust between the participants very slowly. We found that the trust-building exercises were excellent and it did not take long for the atmosphere to become one of acceptance, mutual support, trust and appreciation. This was the only way to ensure that the participants did not approach the subjects judgementally. Instead they learned to relax and listen to what their inner voices told them and to what the others were telling them.

At the same time, the incredible variety of people within the groups meant that the Appreciative Inquiry and Storytelling stages were very exciting and productive.

Language

The linguistic ability within the groups was also a challenge. This was especially true for the English-speaking group, as for the majority of the participants English was not their mother tongue. We managed to achieve a relatively smooth process as the participants supported each other and they also had the help of the organisational team. However, the language problem was outweighed by the multitude of cultures from three different continents that aided the workshops positively. The organisational team had the help of simultaneous translators for the Spanish and French workshops.

We found it imperative to define common terms that we were using during all three workshops. We looked at the terms "family" or "leader" for example and tried to find out what they meant to each participant.

What is my knowledge worth?

When you demand that people divulge their knowledge, it can often fail for the simple reason that they do not know what is relevant for other people or even how much their knowledge is worth. Many people are convinced that the experiences they have gathered are not of interest to anybody else. In order for people to be able to learn how to mobilise their own knowledge, you have to convince them that their experiences are interesting and important, and that they are successful, because they act according to what they know in combination with using their intuition.

Gathering and telling stories

The Harvesting participants told their success stories about subjects such as prevention work or leadership. They chose situations where they proved themselves and where they had the full support of their teams. The space they were given to tell stories and to listen to the others created an almost explosive need to recount their stories and to use their own creative potential. Everybody found original ways to express what could only be felt as emotions or strengths and to articulate them to make them understandable for the others, be it through the use of pictures, artistic interludes or reports.

The groups had to be reminded constantly to see the individual statements made in the context of the whole organisation so that the appreciation phase did not end up being too self-appraising or just a list of anecdotes. We managed to do this during the storytelling and gathering phase because, "what is really exciting ...is how many people truly believe in our organisation" (Anonymous Harvesting participant). This meant that we had a highly emotional rudder which prevented deviations.

Tiredness

Despite the fact that the workshops were highly varied, revolving as they did around Appreciative Inquiry with its didactic approach of working in small groups, we found that ten days in an unfamiliar environment could be very tiring. In such moments we very consciously "worked with all our senses". The participants determined the topics of the presentations and how to present the information; they moderated the group discussions themselves and saw how challenging it was when they had to work in multilingual groups. They took over the planning of leisure time activities: a spontaneous Venezuelan dance, Indian Pujas in the mornings or just a hearty "cheers" from Ghana that included a thought for the deceased. One evening, for example, all the participants cooked a typical meal from their countries. The hosts either helped with the cooking or were just invited to savour the delicacies.

Location and duration

Following the English and Spanish workshops held in Austria, we decided to bring the whole process geographically closer to the participants. The

French-language Harvesting workshop was therefore held in co-operation with the local co-workers in Morocco.

We therefore had the possibility of comparing and evaluating whether the location of the workshop had any relevant influence on the working processes and the results. This was certainly so:

- The culture shock was not as big during this workshop, which meant we were able to work in a stress-free environment.
- Because the training centre in Morocco was somewhat isolated and the leisure-time programme quite limited, it meant that the participants were forced to concentrate more on the workshop itself
- The group adapted the programme far more to suit its needs. The participants were more active and their work ethic was not all-consuming.
- Both the representatives of the head training facility of SOS Children's Villages were immediately accepted as equal partners at this venue. They were not seen to be in a position of authority.
- The local co-workers were very interested in the training methods used by the head office. They found out a lot about them and immediately integrated them in their regional training scheme.
- The Austrian team learned a lot from the pragmatic approach to the organisation of the workshop in Morocco. Because they were also able to see the challenges the co-workers face in their daily work at first hand, they gained more understanding for the efforts the co-workers have to put in every day.

A network for the time after Harvesting

Natural networks were created during Harvesting through direct, personal exchanges. Because the participants got to know each other well, they will often ask for advice and support from these colleagues in the future. They have already developed a common language and have broken down barriers between themselves so it is much easier to seek help from these people. This network should be used to make personal knowledge available to others in the form of reports, good practice anthologies and exchange forums, as well as to collect knowledge and experiences effectively. Despite the fact that the participants are very far away from one another, they are still exchanging ideas amongst themselves.

One of the exercises carried out during Harvesting to encourage this networking was that the participants had to place reports and photographs on the organisation's intranet every day. They knew that these reports were being read carefully by their colleagues back home.

The harvest

It was well worth the effort and expense that it cost the organisation to free its leading co-workers for 14 days to take part in a structured exchange of experience. The hard work it took to organise and carry out a seminar of this type also paid for itself. The feedback messages have shown that Harvesting not only made its mark on the participants on a personal level, but also affected the team and organisation levels positively. The organisation's top managers requested that the workshop output be made even more user-friendly, which shows that even at the highest hierarchical levels of the organisation, the Harvesting results were being read, valued and considered to be of great importance for the organisation.

The objectives set by top management before Harvesting was developed were achieved:

* Leading co-workers, who had been with the organisation for at least ten years found time and space in the Harvesting workshops to exchange views on the preservation of values and educational topics. The concept of leadership and leading was dealt with in depth.
* The participants were able to return home with a tried and tested method of exchanging knowledge. They are now using these methods in their own workshops and are therefore acting as multipliers. All co-workers can read the reports from the Harvesting workshops. Information is available to everyone both on the methods used and about the main topics.
* It is beyond doubt that our long-standing co-workers found the workshop very motivating. This can be read in the evaluation reports. The fact that the participants are prepared to take responsible positions in all the global strategy groups shows clearly that they have got to grips with the new strategic developments within SOS Children's Villages.

Harvesting has proved and underlined the notion that knowledge is one of the success factors for any organisation providing this knowledge is continually part of the co-workers' awareness; it must be shared, generated and implemented in the organisation's activities.

Further reading

Baacke, Dieter/Schulze, Theodor (1979): Aus Geschichten lernen, Juventa, München.

Berger, Karin (Hrsg.) (1985): Der Himmel ist blau. Kann sein. Frauen im Widerstand. Österreich 1938–1945, Promedia, Wien.

Besser, Ralph (2001): Transfer: Damit Seminare Früchte tragen, Beltz, Weinheim.

Bruck, Walter (2004): Menschenorientierte Unternehmensentwicklung: http://www.wb-consult.de, Bad Homburg.

Cooperrider, David L./Whitney, Diana (o.J.): Indagación Apreciativa. Corporation for positive change, Taos, New Mexico, USA.

Denning, Stephen (2001): The springboard: how storytelling ignites action in knowledge-era organizations, Butterworth Heinemann, Boston, USA.

Denning, Steve (2004): http://www.stevedenning.com/SIN-136-HBR-publishes-Telling-Tales.html.

Frenzel, Karolina/Müller, Michael/Sottong, Hermann (2004): Storytelling. Das Harun-al-Raschid-Prinzip, Carl Hanser Verlag, München, Wien.

Frenzel, Karolina/Müller, Michael/Sottong, Hermann (2005): http://www.system-und-kommunikation.de/relaunch/content/index.php, München.

Hallmayer, Regine (2005): http://www.4managers.de, Rottenburg.

Lamnek, Siegfried (1995): Qualitative Sozialforschung. Band II. Methoden qualitativer Sozialforschung, Beltz Verlagsunion, Weinheim.

Stake, Robert E./Alema, T. (2000): Telling Tales: On Evaluation and Narrative, Jai Press, Stanford, USA.

Titscher, Stefan (Hrsg.) (1998): Methoden der Textanalyse. Leitfaden und Überblick, Westdt. Verlag, Opladen.

Weatherhead Executive Education, Weatherhead School of Management, Case Western Reserve University (2005): Appreciative Inquiry Commons, http://appreciativeinquiry.cwru.edu, Cleveland.

Yiannis, Gabriel (2000): Storytelling in Organisations. Facts, Fictions, and Fantasies, Oxford University Press.

Zur Bonsen, Mathias/Maleh, Carole (2001): Appreciative Inquiry, Beltz, Weinheim.

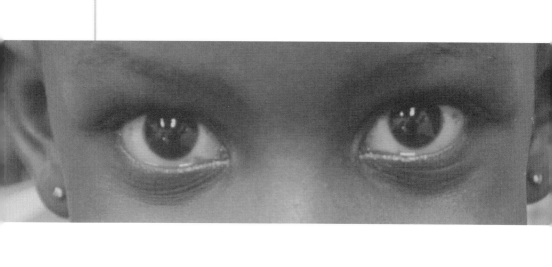

Karin Salchegger

Learning from one another

Setting up and expanding HIV/Aids programmes in Africa

"Just imagine you work for SOS Children's Villages in South Africa. Up to now your work has revolved around the core aspects of the organisation's mission. You have been working at giving long-term care to children in a family-like environment. All of a sudden you are given the task of creating a programme to support HIV/Aids orphans. This is a totally new field for you. What do you do?" These are the questions that Evelyn Winkler asked SOS Children's Village co-workers in Innsbruck. At the time she had been working for SOS Children's Villages in South Africa for 15 months as a knowledge transfer co-ordinator. Her task there was to set up a communication network throughout the SOS Children's Village world. The aim of this network was to provide knowledge and experience from the existing HIV/Aids programmes to the co-workers who were just starting up in this field.

Building SOS Children's Villages will never be enough on its own to deal with the unimaginable suffering of the eleven million children (cf. UNAIDS/ UNICEF 2003) living in Sub-Saharan Africa who have lost either one or both parents.

This challenge requires new methods: the problem of having to care for children can only be solved in the long-term if the aid strategy moves towards strengthening families and communities, allowing them to be able to protect and care for their own children.

Donors are very interested in donating money towards family-strengthening projects. Evelyn, an SOS-Kinderdorf International co-worker, was given the task of gathering information and passing it on to the "right" people. The need to act rapidly and in as many locations as possible was apparent. But the question was, "how?" The answer to that was: through knowledge exchange. That meant documenting the existing experiences and knowledge from the co-workers who were working in family programmes and making this knowledge available for everybody.

The seeds had been sown in SOS Children's Villages' 2003 strategic plan, where family strengthening was first mentioned. Now it had blossomed and "prevention" had become a very important topic.

> **Prevention: Strengthening families so that children are no longer abandoned**
>
> The abandonment of children and the breakdown of families are of global concern and our work has naturally grown into these areas. A clear and aligned prevention strategy throughout the organisation will also respect external child care trends, which donor agencies and potential international NGO partners support. Economically and socially disadvantaged families therefore become a new target group for our work, as it is those families who abandon their children in desperate situations. These families are normally led by young single women living with their children in poverty. As a clearly stated second priority to the SOS Children's Village we will use all our facilities and programmes to actively address the causes that lead to abandonment and help children stay within their families and community (Taking Action for Children, SOS-Kinderdorf International 2002, p. 4).

The organisation set its goal to support 100,000 children, who were living on the edge of society and who were in danger of having to turn to child-labour, forced marriages, prostitution or criminality within the next five years. The bi-annual reports received from the projects have shown that the organisation is on track and that even though the goal was set very high, it will be well exceeded.

In all the SOS Children's Village locations the existing facilities such as SOS Social Centres or SOS Medical Centres should be used for family-strengthening programmes so that more children will be able to enjoy the care of their own families. At the same time, rather than developing one single support model, it would be necessary to develop many different types that are adapted to the differing needs and situations. For example, in South America, it is mostly single mothers who need help to be able to keep their children. In the HIV/Aids affected regions young people are often the ones who take on the responsibility of looking after their younger brothers and sisters. They try to survive in so-called brother and sister households, or they move in with their grandparents, who in turn would actually be dependent on their sons and daughters.

« We have to streamline our work outside of the SOS Children's Villages and put it in a clear pattern. This was the success of the SOS Children's Village movement. With clear and simple principles we will be successful also.» (Family Strengthening Programmes Manual, SOS-Kinderdorf International 2005, p. 1). In order to be able to formulate these models as standards (cf. Standards as the framework for a network, p. 169) we used the

good practice experiences from existing facilities and programmes, both from within the organisation as well as from external projects.

The idea

Now back to Evelyn Winkler, who was working in Innsbruck in 2003 where she was responsible for the flow of information between the head office and the SOS Children's Village facilities in southern and east Africa. She became increasingly aware of the fact that, in order to fully understand the work being carried out in the region, she would have to spend some time there. She notes: "I wanted to learn more about the differences and to understand them. We are one large organisation and have a common vision. I realised that I could only understand the whole picture if I went to work in one of our offices in Africa for a while."

There was a growing awareness within the senior management of SOS Children's Villages that we had to see ourselves as a "learning" organisation in which the need for knowledge exchange had become acute. Senior management realised that unless resources were put in place, it would not be possible to carry out a targeted transfer of knowledge. This led to the creation of a new position, namely that of a knowledge transfer co-ordinator. The organisation also realised that something needed to be done urgently to support the establishment and expansion of HIV/Aids programmes in Africa.

In order to support the future knowledge transfer co-ordinator, the organisation looked at other experiences that had been made in this field in other projects. "I was given the task of setting a process in motion about which I had very little knowledge or experience. I didn't want to reinvent the wheel and so we decided to gather all the existing knowledge we had in the field from within the organisation. In order to learn and to make my task easier, I turned to my colleagues who had experience in such things. I now 'preach' this principle in my job as a knowledge-transfer co-ordinator in South Africa: Look around you! Find out where these things have been done before; who has information or documents on the subject? Who can you learn from before you start a new support programme?"

The organisation possesses a wealth of diverse experience, but our rapid growth promoted a culture that emphasises 'acting instead of talking'. Experience and knowledge is shared informally, instead of being made widely available. A holistic approach to experience and knowledge is now necessary to allow us to develop a learning culture and more quickly share knowledge leading to improvements in the way we work. (…)The need to establish core principles for knowledge sharing is evident across all strategic initiatives. Methods of identifying, documenting and sharing knowledge will be studied and concrete actions determined (Taking Action for Children, SOS-Kinderdorf International 2002, p. 19).

The knowledge transfer workshop

During the winter of 2003/2004 a working group evaluated three of the projects being carried out by the Hermann Gmeiner Academy that were particularly useful for supporting the work of the knowledge transfer co-ordinator: Good Practice Workshops, Harvesting and Tracking Footprints.

The group was made up of an external consultant, whose task it was to help put together an evaluation framework, three members of each of the project teams and the future knowledge-transfer co-ordinator. This working group formulated the following aims for a knowledge transfer workshop:

- The co-workers working on each of the projects should extract any relevant knowledge and put the lessons they had learned at the disposal of the future knowledge transfer co-ordinator.
- Any new knowledge arising from the evaluation of the projects should be made available to help improve current or future projects.
- Develop new tools or bases for the transfer of knowledge.
- At the end of the workshop there should be a short, easy to read report in which the fields of knowledge are clearly defined, the lessons learned are included in an abbreviated form, and concrete steps for implementation are listed.

The first step was, with the help of the external consultant, to determine what knowledge transfer would mean for SOS Children's Villages. The goals were defined and specific activities were chosen.

Following this, each participant wrote a knowledge report about his or her project using the structure defined below:

- What information do we have?
- A short project description (aim, which levels of the organisation are involved, project team, duration).
- The results with examples (5 to 10 good practice examples).
- Extract the most important lessons learned and
- Adapt them to make concrete recommendations for the establishment of an HIV/Aids programme.

The five areas of knowledge that were defined for the workshop (collection of good practice experiences, personal exchanges, networking, storytelling and learning from others) were used as a grid to analyse the three projects being used and to develop a method of evaluation to support the process of transferring knowledge to the HIV/Aids programmes. The consultant helped the group to formulate questions about the areas of knowledge that the project teams had to answer in writing. Finally, Evelyn Winkler, in her role as knowledge-transfer co-ordinator, carried out interviews with each of the project teams and wrote a report on each of the five areas of knowledge following the structure given below:

Characteristics of the methods used in the projects:	Description of the context:	How we can re-use the information:
- Short description (typical uses, most important strengths, purpose of these methods, aims) - Challenges/ starting point - Lessons learned - Necessary organisational efforts - Necessary resources/ time - Passing the methods on	- Typical project/ first project - Participants - Characteristics of the knowledge brought in (explicit, implicit) etc.	- Procedures for implementing the results - Tips and tricks - Reservations/risks - Explanatory documents - Contact person for further questions

Table 1   Report structure

These documents were developed further in a final meeting and revised by Evelyn Winkler accordingly. The information was structured for all five areas with the help of the consultant. It was then put at the disposal of all co-workers in the SOS Intranet in the form of a Power Point presentation[1]. The document is also available as a PDF file, which can be downloaded from the internet.[2]

Introduction to each of the five areas of knowledge

Learning from others

Imagine you have been asked to start a new project. You think that other people have probably gone through the same process before. They may not have been working on the same topic, but at least they have 'tried and tested' methods that could be useful for you and could make your work easier. How can I prepare myself so that I am successful in my task and how can I use what others have learned?

Collecting good practice experiences

Imagine you are starting a new project, but you don't know where to begin. You've heard that another colleague has the experience you require. This is a good opportunity to gather the good practice experiences that this colleague has made and to adapt them to your own requirements.

A workshop for the personal exchange of knowledge and good practice experiences

Image that you have to plan a workshop where people are asked to talk about their experiences in certain fields. They might all come from different countries with differing cultures and ways of working. You will need help in order to make this exchange as fruitful as possible.

Networking and getting something new off the ground

Imagine you are starting a new project which will include and affect many people from different departments of the organisation. You've already taken the first steps and have immediately encountered resistance. Maybe your boss is not sure how it is supposed to continue. One day, you will realise that the most important step to take is to talk to the others and to learn from them so that you can develop your project further.

Storytelling

Imagine you are sitting in a boring meeting where your boss has been giving a lecture to the group for over an hour. You start to daydream and see some wonderful pictures. You think there must be a better way of exchanging information amongst colleagues. You've heard that storytelling is a very effective method for gathering knowledge and passing it on.

---

1   The sub-headings for each of the five areas were: Why is this topic important?/Short description/Use of the methods/Tips and tricks/Experts/Further information

2   www.hermanngmeineracademy.org -Transfer of Knowledge – Events

Reflecting on the knowledge transfer workshop

Christina Lechner-Kreidl took part in the knowledge transfer workshop as a representative of the Good Practice Workshops (cf. Chapter 2, The Treasure Chest): "We were faced with a seemingly unsolvable problem. We had to filter out the lessons learned from a whole range of different projects that would be useful in helping the knowledge-transfer co-ordinator to do her job. If Evelyn had already been working in her new job for longer, it would have been easier for us to know what part of our knowledge could be of help. The question as to what information we had that could be used again put us in a real quandary: we found that one particular report could not be used again; however, parts of the document did seem to be useful. We were faced with this dilemma throughout the whole process. Another challenge was that we had to try not to think about the contents of the project, but to concentrate on the process. We found that we were constantly getting tied up in discussions about the content. Without the help of the external consultant, I'm sure we would have got totally lost. The interviews that Evelyn held with each of us gave us the chance to go more deeply into the subject and to complete any of the extracts we'd taken. I found this part very useful. Not only did I have the opportunity to reflect on my own project, but we also saw the processes in a new light. Previously, we felt that we had got lost in the many processes, but now we were able to see that they had been very fruitful."

After working for a year, Evelyn reflected on the process again and looked for anything useful she could gain from it. She realised that it is difficult to determine what actually came out of the workshop and what she had previously known without realising it: "As a newcomer to this field I found that being able to meet my colleagues and ask them to tell me more about their specialised fields and about knowledge transfer gave me a lot of courage and self-confidence. I was given a good overview and a 'practical' introduction into the possible meaning of knowledge transfer as well as how to choose from amongst a whole list of good practice experiences. I have been able to use, without any restrictions, the tips and tricks on how to organise a workshop in general and good practice sharing workshops in particular. I was given a lot of 'gentle' hints on how to build a network group on human resources management, for example, and how to deal with any possible undesired dynamic processes."

What does a knowledge-transfer co-ordinator do?

Evelyn Winkler described an actual example from her daily work in order for us to see what it is she does. A family of brothers and sisters was living in a tumbledown shelter in Qwa Qwa/South Africa. You could hardly even describe the place as a hut. They were barely able to get enough to eat let alone think about going to school. Their mother had died of Aids a few years previously; their father had found a job in another part of the country and, as so many others before him, had started a new family there. He did not want to have to provide financially for his children from his first marriage any more than he had to. Every now and then he would send them a bit of money. The four brothers and sisters were dependent on handouts that mostly came from their neighbours.

The SOS Social Centre in Qwa Qwa became aware of the untenable situation that these children and youths were living in. As a so-called ,child headed household' they had to fend for themselves. The head of the project decided to use a simple but effective means of helping the children. She knew that the children were entitled to receive financial support from their father as well as orphan benefit payments. She was able to get both for the brothers and sisters by explaining to their father that what he was doing was against the law and she was prepared to fight for the rights of his children. They did not have to go to court. The children now receive a regular maintenance payments of twelve euros every month from their father instead of, as previously, twelve euros per year. In addition the head of the project applied for benefits for the children as half-orphans after the father provided the necessary papers for the authorities and all the forms had been filled out. Finally, the father also helped his children to build a solid hut with two rooms and cooking and washing facilities. Now the children are able to go to school again.

It is this type of success story that the knowledge-transfer co-ordinator has to make available as good practice example to as many co-workers in family-strengthening programmes as possible.

An ideal yet utopian situation for the transfer of knowledge would be if it would occur automatically. In terms of the cost and time involved automatic and unhampered knowledge transfer would be the best. However, in reality we have seen that co-workers often lack the time or do not take the time to turn their experiences into illustrative stories that could be useful to pass

on to others. This would mean that SOS Children's Villages would need their own co-workers whose sole task would be to deal with passing on knowledge. The knowledge-transfer co-ordinator is one of them. It is her task to do the following for the programme in the SOS Social Centre in Qwa Qwa:

- To write up information and put it at the disposal of others (**documenting good practice experiences**),
- To ensure that exchanges can take place between experts (**peer-to-peer exchanges about field visits**),
- To ensure that exchanges about good practices can be gathered in workshops – for example: how long will the children receive support from the SOS Social Centre in Qwa Qwa? Would they have had any chance of winning a legal battle against the father? (**Organisation of Good Practice Workshops**),
- To pass on information that can be used for the whole organisation, regardless of regional or continental borders, to support the initiative "Prevention of child abandonment: strengthening the family" (**construction of a network**).

Simple is not simple enough – Documenting good practice experiences

The aim is clear: the existing, positive practical examples should be written up in a short, simple and understandable format. They should encourage others to use these methods, but at the same time should also draw the reader's attention to any possible stumbling blocks so that time, money and nerves can be saved by avoiding the same mistakes. As simple as this sounds, in reality it cannot be taken for granted that documents like this are actually written. The people who work in the field of social services tend not to take the time to reflect on and structure their experiences. People will take the time to write down their experiences when they realise that this is not just a bureaucratic exercise – or a waste of paper that will simply lie around in a desk drawer somewhere but rather that these documented good practice examples may be able to help other colleagues. However, the next problem is that a certain amount of experience and certain skills are necessary to enable co-workers to produce a useful document. This is where the help and support of a knowledge-transfer co-ordinator is needed. It is her job to provide simple guidelines that everybody can follow: for example, the document should not be longer than two pages; it should include names, contact details, explanations, the most important experiences made, tips, suggestions, graphics, symbols or photographs to make it as simple and easy to read as possible (cf. the practical example in the appendix).

Evelyn has put all her skills and efforts into creating generalised documents. Co-workers in the organisation now have access to an easily understandable, well-structured collection of good practice examples. This would not have been possible without Evelyn's hard work. She collected information when visiting and interviewing people who work in the programmes. The more she was able to gain knowledge in the field and prepare herself, the easier it was to observe the day-to-day reality in the field and to be able to put this information into a useful order. She formulated a simple questionnaire with such questions as: How did you start? Why did you decide to pursue this path? In your experience, what were the advantages and disadvantages? If you had to do this again, what would you change? What recommendations can you make for your colleagues who are going through the same process?

She used this information to document the good practice experiences and invited those in charge of the programme to check what she had written.

Lessons learned

- *These documents are mainly being used for training new programme co-ordinators and for internal 'marketing' purposes. They explain what the family-strengthening programme is all about. They are also useful for external needs, for example when we need to inform people of what we, as an organisation, are doing in the field of family and neighbourhood work.*
- *The transfer of knowledge by writing and reading documents has its limitations. The best way to exchange knowledge is still to meet in person.*
- *The good practice documents need to be short and precise.*
- *The collection needs to be put into computer format (intranet, data base), so that it can be regularly updated. This will require more human resources*
- *The documents should be checked by an outsider, preferably somebody who is going to be using the documentation.*

Good Practice Workshops "Family-strengthening programmes"

A continental workshop now takes place every year for the whole of Africa. The navigators[3] whose task is to implement the family-strengthening programme and the programme co-ordinators take part. At the same time the programme co-ordinators from each region also meet once a year. The contents of the workshop are made up of a mixture of orientation work (Where does the organisation want to go? What are the foreseeable developments within the family-strengthening programme?) and the transfer of knowledge (information and discussions about the existing programmes, evaluation of current activities, development of new projects).

| Lessons learned

- *It is necessary to inform the upper management level clearly about the emphasis of the workshops and what fields of experience are of interest for the forum. If this is not done, the management often chooses people to attend the workshops who are not really suitable for this function.*
- *In order to be able to form a group the participants need to have a common identity. This sometimes has to be created at the workshop itself.*
- *Not all methods can be implemented everywhere. Some methods that have been successful in some settings do not automatically work well elsewhere.*
- *At times informal exchanges can be just as productive as formal meetings. It is important to leave enough time for this - fewer formal points on the agenda can sometimes lead to more results.*
- *Having the expert support of experienced co-workers is an enrichment for every workshop.*
- *Having experts from other organisations as guest speakers gives our co-workers an insight into how others do it.*
- *Groups with little or no experience of implementing a workshop need the guidance, advice and help of the knowledge transfer co-ordinator.*

---

3   Navigators are co-workers from all levels of the SOS Children's Village organisation, who apart from carrying out their own job, are responisble for ensuring that the strategic initiatives are carried out and that the goals are reached.

Face-to-face – Peer-to-peer exchanges

Bringing together partners from the same hierarchy level of the organisation so that they can learn from one another is a simple and therefore effective idea. However, this can only work when the chemistry between the partners is right and if the contents of the exchanges are useful for both parties. The balance between giving and taking must be as equal as possible. The exchanges can take part on any hierarchy level. Including the management levels from the outset helps to avoid any misunderstandings and secures acceptance for the exchanges as well as the necessary resources.

Before one partner visits the other's working place, it is useful to prepare a simple information pack about the programme as an initial orientation. A useful method is to allow the visitor to help with the actual work being done. It is also constructive to take written notes on important realisations, unanswered questions and follow-up procedures. A mentor programme should follow on from the first meeting. An experienced programme co-ordinator who has already successfully planned and implemented a programme should accompany a new and inexperienced co-ordinator for a certain amount of time and work together with him or her in setting up a new programme.

Lessons Learned
• *These peer exchanges can be very useful for new co-workers as part of their orientation.* • *It helps to have guidelines for the exchange: how far are we with the programme, what practical steps do we need to cover during the exchange and what results do we expect?*

A network of knowledge

The organisation appointed regional navigators for each of the topics in the new strategy. Their task was to implement the decisions made by top management regarding the transfer of knowledge and put them into practice in the real world (cf. Chapter.1, Let the flowers grow). The navigators invest a certain amount of time and energy in projects like establishing the family-strengthening programmes. However, they only have a consultative function and are not able to make any decisions themselves.

| Lessons learned

- *An ambitious project like the family-strengthening programme requires a navigator who can concentrate fully on the tasks involved (full-time).*
- *A navigator needs to be able to make decisions. Otherwise he only has limited powers to act.*
- *All the knowledge transfer activities should be integrated into the current structures.*

The appointment of a **knowledge-transfer co-ordinator** to assist the continental navigators in organising knowledge transfer activities has so far only happened in Africa where the HIV/Aids pandemic demands quick action. It is here that the setting-up and expanding of family-strengthening programmes needs a lot of support. Douglas Reed is the navigator for Africa and the Near East. He emphasised that, "The transfer of knowledge is especially important where it does not happen as a matter of course: between the different countries. The real challenge lies in being provided with enough staff and resources to promote the development across the whole continent. Even if at first I wasn't too sure what to expect from a knowledge transfer co-ordinator, what I did know was that I needed all the support I could get to collect the good-practice examples on the one hand, and on the other to make sure that they were then passed on to the right people. Now, after working together for 15 months, I have a much better idea of what knowledge transfer means and how we can bring it about. A knowledge transfer co-ordinator can find the best way to transfer knowledge within very specific organisational situations."

| Lessons learned

- *All the key managers - from the international level down to the regional level - need to have a clear idea about what the transfer of knowledge is and how important the role of a knowledge-transfer co-ordinator is.*
- *His or her role must be explained to the respective management levels (for example, the continental directors) so that they can understand and support this person in their work.*
- *The post of a knowledge-transfer co-ordinator should only be required for a limited time. The co-worker in this position should get the ball rolling and pave the way for the transfer of knowledge. It should not become a permanent position. The ideal situation will have been reached when the transfer of knowledge has become an integral part of all the work being carried out.*

The regional advisors for the family-strengthening programmes, who are responsible for putting these programmes into action, are especially important for the network. In order to maintain a certain level as regards the contents of the information, we found that it proved effective to include the continental navigator in the orientation phase for new consultants. We need to project the idea that knowledge transfer is an enrichment of our co-workers' tasks and not an extra job to do. The section of the job-profile that includes the promotion and organisation of knowledge-transfer needs to be emphasised more. The value of a knowledge-transfer culture should be communicated clearly to new co-workers. Our experience shows that if this is not done, the part of the job that involves the transfer of knowledge tends to be neglected.

All seven navigators for the family-strengthening programmes and the knowledge-transfer co-ordinator come together twice yearly at the continental network meetings. During these meetings they interpret the management's instructions in a continental context, give them practical recommendations and ensure that the topic of family-strengthening programmes is also included as one of the main points in the agenda at other meetings. The consultants for the family-strengthening programmes are given a good overview of the "market" at these network meetings: who has developed what and where there are good practice experiences that all the co-workers in Africa could benefit from.

| Lessons learned

- *The network meetings are useful forums for meeting people for the first time and for keeping in touch with others.*
- *We should send out regular information so that the network members have the feeling they are part of a "team". If we ask for contributions and/or feedback on a regular basis, this builds up trust.*
- *No decisions should be made on a wider organisational level nor should any information be sent out without first clearing it with the network.*
- *If the organisation's management receives recommendations from a network, this is more convincing than if they receive it from one person alone.*

Standards as the framework for a network

At the same time as the SOS Children's Village Manual was being written, the standards for the family-strengthening programmes were also being developed. One of the main differences was that the SOS Children's Village Manual was based on fifty years of practical experience, whereas the family-strengthening programmes were just in the starting blocks. At the time they were not yet understood by everyone, nor had their standards been discussed on a broader basis.

The six family-strengthening programme standards

1. Our programmes are targeted at the most vulnerable children
2. We ensure that families have access to essential services for the child
3. We support families to build their capacity to protect and care for their children
4. We support communities to respond effectively to the situation of vulnerable children and their families
5. We work together with partners to achieve common goals
6. The design and development of programmes ensures that they are relevant and effective. (Family-Strengthening Programmes Manual-Discussion Paper, SOS-Kinderdorf International 2005, p. 7)

In order to make each of the standards easily understandable we used the good practice examples. This is also a good opportunity to inform people about the manual for the family-strengthening programmes. After all, in order to be able to decide whether your own project is a good practice example, you need to know what the standards are. Each programme is evaluated and assessed on the basis of these standards: what areas have been successful? Where do we still need to improve in order to implement these standards?

How the position might develop

It is still too early to draw any final conclusions. The position of knowledge-transfer co-ordinator was originally planned for one year. This has already been extended by a further year. She has set the idea of the transfer of knowledge in motion, but it still has to gain its own momentum. The initiatives that have been started over the past few months still need some time until they become fully self-sustained in the future.

Although Evelyn Winkler has collected experiences with each of the four knowledge transfer tools described (documentation, peer-to-peer exchanges, Good Practice Workshops and the network), documentation is the method she has grown most familiar with. Despite the simple and abridged guidelines for producing documents, she still has to spend a lot of time re-writing the contributions she receives in order to be able to formulate clearly understandable and generalised descriptions of the programmes. It may be necessary in future to have a co-worker whose sole task it is to rewrite the contributions.[4] Douglas Reed would rather have the programme co-workers doing this work themselves: "The people who write these documents should be the ones who use them too!" The following feedback which we received about the documentation of a knowledge transfer process proves this point: "I needed to know how other SOS Children's Village programmes deal with volunteer helpers: are they given financial compensation? Are these programmes run by the communities or by the SOS Social Centres? And so on. I got in touch with the contact persons mentioned in the good practice report, who were already working with volunteers and found out how they deal with them. I was especially interested in a project where SOS Children's Villages was working together with volunteers from another organisation. I found this information very helpful and I think it would be a good idea if my programme co-ordinator could spend a week looking at the project in more detail as part of a peer-to-peer exchange."[5]

The strongest argument for transferring knowledge across the continent of Africa is the very development of the family-strengthening programme. The goals set by senior management of SOS Children's Villages will be well exceeded. Our careful estimates show that they will probably be exceeded by at least 25%. Our optimistic estimates suggest we might even have exceeded our objectives by as much as 50%.

---

4   This experience was made with the "good practice database" in the SOS Intranet. We found that unless there is somebody whose job it is to prepare the examples, the database is not really useful.

5   Extract from a regional navigator's feedback (Africa), 2005.

Appendix

Excerpt from the "Good-Practice-Report for Family-Strengthening Programmes Bindura", Zimbabwe (cf. Winkler, SOS-Intranet)

Programme Description

SOS Children's Villages in Bindura, Zimbabwe has been running a family-strengthening programme since April 2003. The programme aims at providing holistic care for children who have lost one or both parents or are living with terminally ill parent(s) in two of Bindura's high-density areas (Chipadze and Chiwaridzo). The programme started to operate from the SOS Children's Villages site, however then moved into the community of Chipadze where a former SOS youth facility has been renovated to accommodate the social centre facility. The programme renders support to about 1200 vulnerable children in the following four areas:

Health: access to basic medical services, psychosocial support, supplementary food, voluntary counselling and testing, nutrition model garden, medicinal herb garden, hygiene workshops;

Education: support with school fees, uniforms and school material, guided talent development programme, life skills training through recreation and culture, community play group;

Accommodation: legal advice and assistance to obtain legal documents (e.g. birth/death certificates);

Livelihood: training and support on micro-projects, food-production and security;

Further information contact
Farai Siyachitema-Maruza
Social centre coordinator
+263-23-305452

Relevant standard and good practice

We ensure that families have access to essential services for their children
  * support package is tailored to meet the basic survival and development needs of the child in a holistic manner.

Description

For children to become enrolled onto our programme, they need to fulfil the following criteria:
  * Double orphan or living with chronically ill parent(s) or abandoned for more than five years
  * Below sixteen years of age and willing to attend formal school
  * Resident in the designated area for at least six months
  * No significant benefits from other organisations
  * Willingness of family/guardian to get involved in self sustainability activities and programmes

In order to prove eligibility of these criteria, birth and death certificates are required. To assist guardians in acquiring these documents, we organise respective legal advice workshops.

Children, who are enrolled in our programme, receive direct assistance in the following areas:
   Nutrition: monthly food-supplements
   Education: payment of school fees, uniforms and school material
   Health: access to basic medical services

Besides these very basic and direct services for the child, we also organise activities that ensure the psychosocial well-being of the children through:
   Mitambo ne Magariro *(recreation and culture)*: regular sports & arts sessions
   Huyai Tionesane (psycho-*social support programme*): six grief work groups for bereaved children and three positive-living support groups for guardians have been formed.

In the absence of appropriate child care facilities, the need for a crèche for pre-primary school children became evident. So, parents and community members were mobilized to establish a day-care centre. The Salvation Army School provided a building. One of the SOS staff members is a former kindergarten teacher and as such was able to train five interested, volunteer guardians to hold kindergarten sessions for about 60 children. It should be noted, that this day-care centre is being set-up and is running on donations, contributions and support by the community. It does not receive any financial input from the SOS Social Centre, apart from staff and transport costs.

Key lessons learned

- Besides material support it is crucial to strengthen the psychosocial support for the children to help them deal with trauma and bereavement and to harmonize the relationship between the guardian and the child.
- The community day-care centre project proves that it is possible to mobilize community members to run a programme without major financial input from the SOS organisation.

Relevant standard and good practice

We support families to build their capacity to protect & care for their children.
- A comprehensive support package, based on local needs and the specific family circumstances is developed to gradually lead the family towards self-reliance.

Description

At the beginning of our programmes' operation, we focused mainly on meeting the immediate survival and development needs of the children by giving them material, educational and medical assistance. However, during the second year of our operations, we designed specific programme activities, based on the needs of our participating families to develop skills and capacities to gradually lead the families towards self-reliance. These are the underlying principles which we use to encourage and motivate our beneficiary families:

- **Start** where you are.
- **Start** with what you have.
- **Start** with the people you know.
- **Start** with what you enjoy.
- **Start** small,
- But for heaven's sake get started! Chekumirira ndopasina! (There is nothing to wait for)

Material and financial self-sufficiency is build through the following activities:
- Mabasa Epundutso *(= micro projects and livelihood support)*: SOS helps to organise and group family members with specific business ideas and then provides relevant training and linkages with relevant partners to realize these ideas. So far a sewing group (uniform making) as well as a building and construction group has been formed. SOS is there to advise and guide the new entrepreneurs, e.g. currently we are supporting the sewing group as they are putting together a funding proposal to the American Embassy.

- Zadzamatura *(= food production and security programme)*: In trade of food parcels, maize seeds and fertilizer were given to families interested in farming and who had the necessary access to a piece of land. The public association AREX (Agriculture Research and Extension) provides technical support in promoting sound agricultural practices.
- Mushandimai *(= home products skills development)*: workshops for guardians were held to teach them how to make lotion, floor polish, jam, Soya meatballs, and other home products.

Taking into consideration the reality, that many of our guardians for the children are terminally-ill, a **health support programme** has been put in place, which consists of several components:

- Voluntary counselling and testing: in cooperation with medical partners
- Nutrition and medical herb garden: a model garden at the social centre was established to conduct workshops on how to grow healthy food and the use of herbs
- Hygiene workshops
- Three positive-living support groups were formed

Key lessons learned

- Self-empowerment strategies have to be designed based on the local needs and the families specific circumstances.
- Each SOS field worker is assigned activities of specialisation to manage. Although the staff members might not have relevant expertise in the assigned area in the first place, but if they bring great interest and passion, they are given respective training to develop in their specific area.
- When working on the grass-root level, the use of the local language is essential to ensure real ownership of the activities. As such, all our activities were given a Shona name.

Key people

The programme is run by 4 fieldworkers, 1 bookkeeper, 2 ancillary staff members and headed by a programme coordinator. The staff members are coming from diverse professional backgrounds (social work, teaching, community development) which ensure a lot of dynamism and creativity within the programme. However, what unites them is their common passion for bringing about changes to the lives of orphans and vulnerable children as well as a very practical and hands-on attitude towards the programmes development.

Social centre staff members

Rüdiger Reinhardt

Suggestions and recommendations for profit-making companies

The previous articles contained in this volume have made it clear how SOS Children's Villages has successfully implemented knowledge communication from both a strategic and an operational perspective. This chapter will discuss to what extent profit-making companies can learn from the experiences and methods of the knowledge communication projects in a non-profit organisation in order to optimise their own processes of knowledge transfer.

In order for this subject to be more easily understood, it is first necessary to define some of the concepts that constitute "knowledge communication". On the one hand these definitions show the differences between exchanging information and exchanging knowledge. On the other hand they also give us the necessary framework in order to give a brief sketch of knowledge communication.

Today we normally refer to "knowledge communication" when we are talking about the tools and methods of knowledge management. We also very often talk about "knowledge exchange", "knowledge diffusion", "knowledge sharing" and "knowledge transfer".

Apart from the fact that the redistribution of knowledge is regarded as being the most difficult phase of knowledge management (Probst et al. 2000, p. 165), there are also many different definitions of both "knowledge transfer" and "knowledge communication" due to the fact that there are various theories and practical problems that must be dealt with.

On the basis of the theoretical analysis in their book, Reinhardt and Eppler (2004, p. 25) see knowledge communication as the (most) deliberately interactive construction of and passing on of experiences, insights and skills on both verbal and non-verbal levels.

This broad definition of knowledge communication goes much further than understanding knowledge as a primarily cognitive phenomenon and interprets it as a social phenomenon that arises through personal interaction. Only then can it develop its full potential. Both emotions and the social context are seen as being significant parts of experiences, insights and skills (cf. also Polanyi 1967). These factors are especially important if knowledge is to be communicated effectively.

Even though knowledge can be communicated without the explicit intention to do so (for example, when people work together) we will focus on the topic of deliberately steering knowledge communication that aims to achieve specific (mostly work-related) objectives. This manner of communication requires interaction, if the knowledge is to be extracted and transferred. In order for the "recipient" to be able to reconstruct the knowledge he has gained, he has to be able to both make sense of and create a context for that knowledge. This is best achieved if it is done together with the "knowledge-provider". Here we understand "knowledge" to be the total sum of insights that people use to solve problems (cf. Probst et al. 2000). It can either be analytical knowledge or knowledge based on experience, i.e. the sense of "know-why" and "know-what", but it can also be procedural knowledge, i.e. "know-how".

In this way, we can see that knowledge communication is much more than the mere transfer of information. The differences between these two are shown in the table below:

Communicating information ...	Communicating knowledge ...
...mostly answers the questions: what, where, where from, when and how much?	...mostly answers the questions: how, why, what will happen if?
... can often be independent of the person or the context.	... requires the context and one's own perspective to be explained.
... can be wrong.	... may be unsuitable rather than wrong.
... has to be provable (e.g. by giving sources).	...needs to be elucidated and motivated much more strongly, as knowledge is also always "an expectation".

Table 1   Comparing two types of communication

In summary we have to emphasise that knowledge communication can neither be planned nor carried out on the basis of a "mechanical" understanding of processes of change nor can it only be realised on the basis of economic measures. If we want to be successful, we need to ensure that a suitable emotional and social framework has been created in which knowledge communication can flourish. In addition, we must take into consideration that any forms of exchanges such as workshops, meetings, etc. require lengthy feedback processes. Without these, there is no way of ensuring that a common understanding of "know-why", "know-what" and "know-how" that is relevant for the organisation has been generated.

Analysis of the projects

In the following section we will analyse each of the individual knowledge transfer projects that SOS Children's Villages has carried out. In our analysis we will extract the lessons learned from these projects that might be useful for profit-making companies. To ensure that the following section is as clear and understandable as possible, we will:

- give a summary of the aims of each of the projects
- identify the critical success factors
- extract the lessons learned on the basis of each of the critical success factors

Good Practice Workshops as a method of quality assurance in SOS Children's Villages

Among the aims of the Good Practice Workshops were:

- To construct a reliable platform for the exchange of good practice experiences supporting the standards in the SOS Children's Village Manual,
- to support a culture of knowledge communication, of learning and of innovation throughout the whole SOS Children's Village organisation, and
- to optimise the implementation of the SOS Children's Village Manual by developing plans to do so on each level of the organisation.

We can see to what extent these aims were achieved through a brief, analytical evaluation of the critical success factors:

Integration into the strategic framework

The main starting point for the Good Practice Workshops was to link the project closely with the organisation's strategic framework. This framework had long been accepted within the organisation. The intention was to relate the implementation of the SOS Children's Village Manual with the exchange of good practice experiences. This was also the most successful part of the Good Practice Workshop as it meant that the senior management's belief in the project led to it being readily accepted by all the participants. They were able to see that the project made sense for those it was going to affect.

The implementation and project management philosophy

The project was imbued with the principle of "turning those affected" into "participants". The high level of participation was not just an important prerequisite in order to identify relevant good practice examples instead of "just any" examples. It also meant that it was easier to apply the good practice examples, having previously been able to modify them. This avoided the erection of a defensive barrier against them, as well as the "it wasn't invented here" syndrome.

The relevance to real life

The workshops concerned themselves solely with identifying "good practice" experiences not "best practice" ones. This meant that the project was valid and realistic for everybody as there was no need to justify why an experience should be judged as "best".

Fears about relinquishing their value and power by giving away the tricks of the trade were easily allayed. This was because so much emphasis was placed on the individual and local relationships to each of the good practice examples.

Communication methods

Despite the complexity of the organisation (132 countries, 458 SOS Children's Villages), the preferred method for exchanging good practice experiences is the "face-to-face" method. The advantages are obvious: if you are talking to somebody personally, you can ask questions and develop what you have been told further. This creates a deeper common understanding and avoids misunder-

standings. Furthermore, personal contact also creates trust, and strengthens the constructive forum necessary for exchanging information.

Quality control and evaluation
What was very apparent during the entire project was the intense awareness of the quality of the project: right from the start it was ensured that the good practice experiences could be identified within the framework of the standardised processes and could thus be used as a basis for a comparison of their relevance. Questionnaires were used to evaluate the preparation phase, the quality of the workshop and the effect that the results had on the work being done in the field. These were filled out before, during and after the workshop.

Documentation and clarity of the results
The results of the workshop were documented in detail so that they would be comprehensible when it came to putting them into practice. The documentation included:

* all the good practice experiences that had been presented and further developed in the continental workshop
* the input on the topics of "knowledge management" and "Good Practice Sharing"
* the general guidelines that had been worked out for the implementation of the SOS Children's Village Manual (implementation plan)
* the evaluation report on the workshop
* the minutes of the workshop.

Documenting a process as comprehensively as this has the advantage that it is interesting for everybody. It clarifies the whole process and, therefore, people can identify with the results and are more eager to implement them.

Dealing with intercultural differences
The final success factor that we will mention is the professional manner in which the topic of "intercultural differences" was dealt with. These differences were included in the project design, and allowed for the good practice experiences to be adapted to suit the unique character of each continent.

Critical success factors	Recommendations for profit-making companies
Strategic integration	You must ensure that your knowledge communication project can be integrated into existing, successful and accepted projects, processes or strategies!
Implementation	The more the people who are involved are included in the implementation of the project, the easier it will be. Take into account that you will be far more successful in achieving your goals if you use the principle of turning "those who are affected" into "participants".
Relevance and feasibility	You can be certain that there will be varying opinions within your organisation on the general feasibility of projects that bring about change. Make sure that the expectations remain realistic. You should also remain modest and realistic. If necessary, you should remain understated. You must certainly take into consideration the various preconditions within which you have to implement the results. If necessary, you should get expert help.
"Face-to-face" communication	If the context is clear and the players trust each other, knowledge communication will be successful. You must ensure that there is as much and varied personal exchange as possible. Do not forget that it takes time to build trust and a deeper understanding of other people's opinions.
Intercultural differences	Never take it for granted that a solution that has been found to be successful in one country will automatically be successful in another. This is not only the case for knowledge communication, but in general for all management methods.
Evaluation and controlling	You can determine whether your project was as successful as intended by using suitable standards and evaluation criteria. Support the use of systematic project-controlling and evaluation methods. These will give your project relevance. You need to deal with the exhaustive spectrum of behaviour in the processes of knowledge communication.
Documentation	You must take into consideration that information technology makes it easier to access the documents. It is important to provide a template that can be used for all documents. You should not forget that it might also be necessary to contact the author directly.

Table 2   Good Practice Workshops – Recommendations for profit-making companies I

Tracking Footprints – local research, global networking

Tracking Footprints is the first long-term, international research project that SOS Children's Villages has carried out. It studied the experiences of people who had not been able to grow up with their own families and had instead grown up in SOS Children's Villages. There were three main questions in this international research and evaluation study: "How are our ‚clients' doing? Are we doing our job properly? How can we improve?"

The following evaluation will show this project's critical success factors. We will show how important it is to have successful knowledge communication in an organisation when carrying out research projects as complex as this one. More than 60 people work on the project, over 1,100 people were interviewed in more than 20 countries. We will also show how the results of this research project were successfully transposed within the organisation. This set off a process of learning and improvement.

The scientific approach

The first thing we noticed about this project was the high standard of the scientific approach. The exemplary quality of this project was shown by the methodically and clearly defined samples taken. A questionnaire was developed which contained several sections (incl. feedback). The interviewers were well prepared and well trained.

It depends very much to what extent one can hold back one's own subjective outlook and look at the project with as neutral a perspective as possible as to how valid and useful the results of such a project are. The quality of this project was ensured by including a "critical friend", an external consultant with experience in intercultural research know-how, external persons in each country who carried out the interviews and external researchers who helped with the evaluation of the questionnaires.

The intercultural nature

What was important here was that the decision was made to use a single questionnaire in which the intercultural differences would not be distorted. Providing a short set of guidelines ("assistant") solved the seemingly contradictory nature of having only one questionnaire for all countries. This assistant explained the questions and allowed the interviewers to deal with them according to national and cultural values.

The implementation and project management philosophy
This project was also implemented along the same lines as the Good Practice Workshops, namely using the principle of turning those affected into participants. One of the most important conditions required was the high standard of participation. This was necessary to ensure enough commitment during the planning and implementation phases.

Workshop
Important platforms for knowledge communication and for creating a network amongst the participants were the Tracking Footprints workshops. The main aims were to provide the project steering team and the people working on the project in the countries with a common understanding of the research being undertaken. They were also used to prepare the participants for their future tasks.

Furthermore, the external interviewers were trained at the workshops. They were given practical examples to work on and then went on to carry out the questioning in their countries.

Documentation and standardisation
The project steering partners documented the research process by using key questions and report sheets. This supported the exchange of experience and knowledge. Members of the project team systematically compared their documentation to ensure that it was not only the individual who was being served in this process.

Identifying former clients' knowledge
Former clients were interviewed about their experiences on the basis of an analysis tool that had been developed by professionals. During this phase, it was interesting to see that by working closely together with external experts a huge contribution towards further developing the SOS Children's Village work was made.

Evaluation

Other contributory factors towards the usefulness of this project were the fact that the project management provided feedback loops so that they could derive measures from the project and have an opportunity to check them. This also meant that the knowledge that had been identified within the organisation was not lost and could continue to be used in the future.

Critical success factors	Recommendations for profit-making companies
Scientific standards	The usefulness of your research results depends very much on your scientific approach. Make sure that you have the relevant methodological competence (either internally or brought in from outside) to carry out the project.
Ensuring validity	It is impossible to interpret results objectively. Do not rely on your personal impressions or on those of your immediate working environment if you need to interpret results. Bring a number of other professional, critical voices into the interpreting and decision-making process.
Intercultural differences	Do not take it for granted that one solution will suit every country. Remember that within an international project management team you will have many different ways of working and you must ensure that the contents of your research can be adapted to suit all social situations in each country.
Participation	You will be able to reach your goals much more easily if you remember to turn those being affected into participants.
Evaluation	You will only find out if your project has been as successful as it was planned to be if you carry out a high standard of evaluation. Do not just carry out the evaluation at the end of the project. You should do so at regular intervals whilst the project is still on going.
Documentation and standardisation	You can only learn from your project (and it will only be successful) if you document the relevant steps and phases of the projects clearly. Take into consideration that you must implement standards for the documentation and that the documents should be written as soon as possible after the event.

Table 3   Tracking Footprints – Recommendations for profit-making companies II

Harvesting – Gathering experiences for dreams of the future

What has made SOS Children's Villages the success it is today? The Harvesting project's main aim was to delve into this question and to collect experiences from within the organisation. On the one hand the organisation wanted this knowledge to be documented so that it can be passed on to new and future co-workers. On the other hand, it wanted to be able to use this knowledge for the organisation's future plans. The most important individual goals were:

- to have an exchange of experiences based on values and educational topics between long-standing co-workers in leading positions.
- to develop a strategy for spreading the knowledge of these long-standing co-workers (for example, via the SOS Intranet that all co-workers can access world-wide).
- to increase the long-standing co-workers' motivation towards the new strategic direction in which the SOS Children's Village organisation was heading.

The following brief analytical evaluation of the critical success factors will show how these goals were reached:

Integration into organisational and human resources development
"Harvesting" did not just provide a method of knowledge communication. It went far further: it was used as an organisational and human resources development tool that revolved around formal and informal exchanges between co-workers.

Appreciative Inquiry
The central aim of Harvesting was to discover the co-worker's implicit knowledge and to make it explicit, to turn unarticulated knowledge that is dependent on experience into articulated knowledge that is independent of the individual.

One of the main problems for successful knowledge communication is the clarification and communication of implicit knowledge. In the course of the Harvesting project it became clear how important it was to have an awareness that implicit knowledge is very much tied to the individual person and not only to that person's role within the organisation.

The aim was, therefore, to create an environment in which the co-workers were able to be open and where trust could be built up between the partners.

The main success factor here was the use of Appreciative Inquiry. This technique meant that it was not only possible to solve the problem of how to organise exchanges in which the hierarchical and cultural differences no longer mattered. It also made it possible to create a basis for communicating very personal, implicit knowledge by using the storytelling technique. This put the knowledge into context and, by working in small groups, the participants were able to make their knowledge available to a much wider audience.

From personal vision to a plan of action

The participants encouraged each other to develop concrete steps (plans of action) that did not only affect that person's own tasks but which were also of use to the whole organisation and any significant partners. To do this they anchored their individual visions of the future by using real-life examples.

Documentation of the plan of action

The participants themselves were partially responsible for documenting their plan of action: they often took notes – especially during the storytelling phase – and later typed them up on a computer. They completed the documentation by adding photos and videos. The notes were taken very carefully as the participants had to use them to write reports afterwards. These had to be written in three languages and participants often used direct quotations to substantiate their opinions.

The project team has archived all the materials, which can now be found in the SOS Intranet in the form of reports, pictures and daily minutes, etc. Anybody who is interested is welcome to read the material.

Evaluation/sustainability

The potential that was discovered in Harvesting was thoroughly analysed in three feedback loops. The organisation's management and every co-worker can access this information in the SOS Intranet.

Six weeks after the workshop ended the participants wrote reports about the first steps they had taken towards realising the goals and plans that had been set. The first round of feedback on the implementation of their planned projects was received six months after the end of the workshop. A further six months later the participants sent in a short report about the processes and the status of their projects. Each of these feedback loops included sections on the individual, the team and the organisational levels involved.

Critical success factors	Recommendations for profit-making companies
Integration into the organisational and human resources development concept	Knowledge communication projects fulfil their potential use far more effectively when they have been linked to as many established processes and/or functions as possible. Make sure that your knowledge communication projects are not isolated "five-day wonders" but are integrated into processes that are already up and running.
Appreciative Inquiry	The usefulness of knowledge communication all depends on the ability to turn implicit knowledge into explicit knowledge, thereby making it useful for others. You must ensure that you have chosen the most suitable method of knowledge communication.
Storytelling	You must create a suitable environment in which knowledge communication can take place successfully. Ensure that the social and organisational framework is suitable for reaching your aims. Also take into account that it takes time to build up trust. Very often there is not enough time planned into the usual efficient "turbo-workshops" to accommodate such a lengthy process.
Plans of action	Knowledge communication does not take place just for its own sake. It should provide an inventory of methods that will help the organisation to reach its goals more easily. You must ensure that the plans of action are used in any planning process. This must also be supervised and evaluated.

Documentation	You can only learn from your project (and it will only be successful) if you document the relevant steps and phases of the projects clearly. Take into consideration that you must implement standards for the documentation and that the documents should be written as soon as possible after the event.
Different levels and multi-stage evaluation	You will only find out if your project has been as successful as it was planned to be if you carry out a high standard of evaluation. Do not just carry out the evaluation at the end of the project. You should do so at regular intervals while the project is still on going. It is important to note that the different levels of evaluation (individual, team and organisational) not only have different evaluation criteria but the necessary IT support will vary for every level too.

Table 4   Harvesting – Recommendations for profit-making companies III

Learning from one another – Setting up and expanding HIV/Aids programmes in Africa

When SOS Children's Villages started its "Learning from one another – setting up and expanding HIV/Aids programmes in Africa", the family-strengthening programme, it was relatively new territory for them as far as their experience and expertise was concerned. The main task was to facilitate exchanges of experience amongst African countries south of the Sahara. This would involve countries with family-strengthening programmes already in place and countries where programmes still needed to be established.

The following analytical evaluation of the critical success factors from this project will show what was achieved and how project implementation teams went about their task:

Innovation and dealing adequately with problems
The organisation had seen that the existing SOS Children's Village model was not adequate to cope with the incredible increase in the numbers of Aids orphans. Therefore, the SOS Children's Village organisation took the bull by the horns and developed and implemented a new approach within

the new strategic framework of the organisation that emphasised the value of knowledge management and communication. A concept was created in order to be able to gather, revise and spread the relevant knowledge required for this problem area.

This innovation caused a shift in paradigms within the organisation away from standardisation to a concept of individualisation. Individualisation was achieved through programmes that were clearly adapted to suit specific needs and situations yet firmly anchored within the standards (guidelines) contained in the Family Strengthening Programmes Manual.

Existing competences and entrepreneurial thinking
One of the most important success factors of this project was that the organisation took the experience they already had internally and used a knowledge transfer process to reflect on this knowledge and to see how it could be used to set up and expand the HIV/Aids programmes in Africa. No less important was the professional approach and the personality of the knowledge transfer co-ordinator. The organisation created conditions that supported both entrepreneurial and personal commitment and the implementation of individual ideas. These ideas were picked out and spread amongst a network of co-workers on the same hierarchy level.

Implementing ideas and learning from experience
The organisation picked out some relevant projects in order to be able to identify the most important experiences so these could be gathered and revised. A working group evaluated three knowledge communication projects together with an external consultant. They sifted out the recommendations for establishing HIV/Aids programmes. At the same time, this process has helped to create new knowledge.

Documentation, standardisation and quality control
The standards in the Family Strengthening Programmes Manual were linked with the structure of the good practice report so that the experiences could be compared. There were good practice examples for each of the standards. Because the documentation had been standardised it was possible to identify the most important experiences and to use them for the HIV/Aids projects.

The advantage of this standardisation also comes to the forefront on the operational side of documenting these experiences. All those involved are helped by being given a simple structure to follow. This makes it relatively easy to compose a document and to place it on the intranet. At the same time, the documents must be proofread and checked by a third person before being published.

External know-how

Learning always implies that you must stand back from your "object of learning". Many profit-making companies make use of external advisors to make unpopular decisions seem legitimate. Despite this danger, SOS Children's Villages has understood how to use an external advisor as a learning partner with whom one can reflect on the problems. The organisation has profited from the consultant's know-how.

The advantages of specialisation

Already at an early stage, the discussion about knowledge management in profit-making companies brought about the creation of special roles – even to the extent of appointing a decision maker (Chief Knowledge Officer). From today's point of view we can see that these attempts at specialisation have mainly failed.

It seems that one positive exception is the role of the "knowledge transfer co-ordinator". Despite the realisation that ultimately knowledge communication is part of the daily work routine of every member of this organisation, the decision was made to create a new role and/or field of work. However, from the beginning it was clear that this role would only be for a limited period of time-for as long as it took to introduce knowledge communication into the tasks and duties of the co-workers. This highlights the fact that the organisation now thinks in terms of long-term strategies rather than in short-term efficiency-boosting measures.

Critical success factors	Recommendations for profit-making companies
Innovation and dealing adequately with problems	If knowledge communication projects are to be successful, all of the stakeholders - on all hierarchy levels of the organisation - have to be willing to learn. You should not be satisfied with what you have achieved so far. You should develop new and innovative solutions and be customer-oriented. Find solutions that solve your clients' and customers' problems and meet their expectations. Do not just find solutions to fit your old habits.
Existing competence and entrepreneurial thinking	Successful changes and innovations can only be achieved if your co-workers are committed and willing to tread new paths and to take risks. Encourage your co-workers to see further than the ends of their noses. Demand entrepreneurial thinking.
Implementing ideas and learning from experience	In order to improve your protagonists' motivation towards processes of change you need to create a suitable basis for implementing these changes. This has to be done as quickly and with as much commitment and follow-through as possible.
Documentation, standardisation and quality control	You can only learn from your project (and it will only be successful) if you document the relevant steps and phases of the projects clearly. Take into consideration that you must implement standards for the documentation and that the documents should be written as soon as possible after the event. Also, do not forget that checking documents against a list of quality criteria or having experts from the same hierarchical level check them will improve the end result.
Using external know-how	Consultants can provide valuable know-how during processes of change. You must ensure that the aims that the consultant is supposed to bring about are made clear to all involved beforehand.
The advantages of specialisation	In order to implement innovative concepts, you might need to create a new function or area of competence. Take a critical look as to how far a new function is really necessary to reach your goals. Do not just look at the (short-term) cost, but instead look at the advantages for the co-ordination and learning factors that a new cross-departmental position would bring with it.

Table 5   Setting up and expanding HIV/Aids programmes - Recommendations for profit-making companies IV

The building blocks of knowledge management

The diagram below shows the various phases, or building blocks, of knowledge management at SOS Children's Villages. We can see clearly that the organisation's knowledge management projects are not just a matter of "dividing up" knowledge. Instead, each phase is relevant for the project.

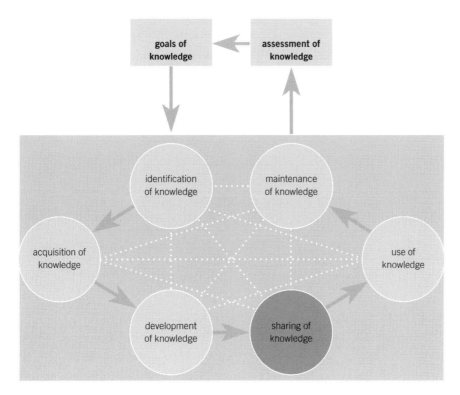

Figure 1   Building Blocks of Knowledge Management (Probst et al. 2000, p. 34)

A perfect example of this can be seen in the Good Practice Workshop project:

Building block	Features of the project purposely taken
Knowledge aims	To create a reliable platform for the exchange of good practice experiences
Identifying knowledge	Identifying the people with the knowledge
Developing knowledge	Developing a basis of knowledge amongst the "receivers" - and thus the organisation
Spreading knowledge	Communicating the knowledge from the people who have it to the receivers
Using knowledge	The receivers use and/or implement the knowledge they have received
Keeping knowledge	Documentation of the results
Evaluating knowledge	Evaluating knowledge with the questionnaires I-III

Table 6   Knowledge communication as an integrated knowledge management concept

What can profit-making companies learn?

There is very little point in conceiving knowledge management projects with relatively one-sided goals – for example, "improving communication" or "improving innovation" – as you usually have to integrate all the building bricks of knowledge management when planning and implementing such projects. **Knowledge management is an integrative concept.**

A great number of useful "side effects" can arise even if a project has been well planned. They might not have been explicitly planned into the process but will nevertheless prove useful. For example, with the project for setting up and expanding HIV/Aids programmes in Africa, there were also aspects of capacity building. Documentation, peer-to-peer exchanges, Good Practice Workshops and the building of a network all led to a lasting development of competences that transcended the scope of the project itself and its direct aims. It was possible to use these competences efficiently, e.g. by the advisor for the family-strengthening programmes or the programme co-ordinators. **Knowledge management is a concept that goes beyond knowledge management.**

What is particularly interesting in this case is the realisation that new and unexpected learning experiences were created through the network of co-workers from all different levels who had come into contact with aspects of knowledge communication. It was possible to put these experiences to good use right across the board of functions and topics. **Knowledge management is the development of networks.**

Operational implications

Table 7 shows an overall view of the critical success factors that were identified in the second section of this paper. Here we can clearly see the common factors found in each of the projects and the operational competences that SOS Children's Villages put to use when implementing each of them.

	Good Practice Workshops	Tracking Footprints	Harvesting	Setting up and expanding HIV/Aids programmes
Implementation	Combine with other strategies Implementation Relevance to real life/ Feasibility		Combining with organisational and human resources development concepts	Dealing suitably with problems, innovation Implementing ideas and learning from experience
Organisational culture, cultural	"Face-to-face" communication Intercultural differences	Participation Intercultural differences		Making use of existing competence/entrepreneurial thinking Using external know-how Specialisation
Project-management	Evaluation and controlling Documentation	Plan of action Evaluation Documentation	Documentation Evaluation on more than one level	Documentation, Standardisation and quality control
Methods and Standards		*Serious scientific approach* − Scientific standards − Ensuring validity	*Problem-specific choice of method* − Appreciative Inquiry − Storytelling	

Table 7   Summary: Success factors and operational competences (cursive) within SOS Children's Villages

The organisational competences listed in Table 7 can be put into concrete terms as follows:

Operational Competence No. 1 – Successful implementation of processes of change: If you can intelligently link your existing processes and/or functions to the new projects being implemented, it will help avoid resistance and/or rejection on the part of the organisation. This will ensure smoother implementation of a new initiative. In addition, you will also be able to create synergies between the old, established processes and the new ones. This has an additional use, in particular when it comes to creating knowledge-intensive values. The various processes, projects and members of the organisation can be linked. Finally we must point out that it is absolutely vital to recognise individual know-how and innovative suggestions in order for your knowledge communication projects to be a success. Clearly, knowledge communication cannot be prescribed. It has to be encouraged by creating the appropriate structures and style of leadership where initiative, innovation and communication can blossom.

Operational Competence No. 2 – Taking into account (organisational) cultural differences: SOS Children's Villages has the competence to deal with intercultural differences respectfully and constructively. This can be put down to the fact that it is a long-standing international organisation whose "business model" – the work in the SOS Children's Villages – is heavily decentralised and has been adapted to suit regional conditions. Thus, the organisation already has a deep understanding of this issue. This explains why the organisational culture is very strongly tied to people. In fact, it would not work if it were any different. It would be unthinkable for the head office of the organisation to set down rules and regulations with the aim of standardising the behaviour of SOS mothers across Africa, Asia, South America or Europe.

Operational Competence No. 3 – Using professional project management methods: The experiences that the industrial world has had with project management over many years have not always been positive. This can be put down to the fact that the project managers have often not been trained adequately, that the co-ordination between project and strategy has not always been clear and finally the almost routine practice of making the best experts the project leaders. What stands out most about the SOS Children's Village projects described in this paper is that the project management's competence is outstanding. Evaluation and project controlling are not seen to be merely tasks that have to be fulfilled. Instead they have been carried out systematically in order to check, correct and improve the project. This is one of the main prerequisites for achieving the best possible success within any project.

Operational Competence No. 4 – Choosing the correct knowledge communication methods: SOS Children's Villages chose specific methods of knowledge communication that were appropriate for the creation of the framework conditions necessary for successful knowledge communication. They took into consideration the emotional and social side of experiences and the manner in which to communicate them. In addition, the choice of methods was in accordance with the main tasks that the organisation carries out. Therefore, the methods are geared towards people. Amongst other things, this shows that – unlike in most profit-making companies – these methods ensure that enough time is spent on building trust and communicating personal experiences during projects.

Operational Competence No. 5 – Taking scientific standards into account: What is of particular interest to an outsider is the use of scientific standards and methodologies in the realisation of these projects. Whereas many commercial enterprises often only make use of experts as an alibi, the projects outlined here clearly show that the scientific advice drawn on was fully intended for use to achieve the best possible results. If scientific methods are used, they must be checked for their validity and their actual usefulness for achieving aims.

Strategic implications

If we take a step back from the projects presented in this book, it becomes clear that they all have strategic importance for SOS Children's Villages. Knowledge communication has the aim here of achieving relevant goals, and/or contributing towards SOS Children's Villages coming one step closer to realising their vision.

Therefore, knowledge communication plays a dual role. On the one hand, it is being used in the projects to optimise implementation and to ensure high quality. On the other hand, knowledge communication is being used as a strategic transmission belt that will ensure the continued success of the SOS Children's Villages organisation in the future.

In these projects knowledge communication serves to process the experiences of people from different groups within the organisation. It is then possible to take into account the success criteria – time, efficiency, quality and orientation towards the co-workers.

When knowledge management projects are carried out in profit-making companies the emphasis is often on operational measures. In contrast, it is not as easy to sift out general recommendations from the SOS Children's Village projects as far as the strategic elements are concerned. However, if we take this difference into account and simply deal with the general experiences of implementing knowledge management projects, we can see the following:

Strategic Competence No. 1 – Using methods that match the core business and procedural models: When we look at the historical development of SOS Children's Villages and the complexity of the organisation today it becomes clear that when making plans, taking decisions and forming actions, the "essence" of the organisation's core business was a guiding factor. The organisation can also only reach its vision of "Every child belongs to a family and grows with love, respect and security" (Who we are, SOS-Kinderdorf International 2002) if the expert and social competences in the field are properly taken into consideration. This can be briefly summarised – at least for organisations whose main tasks lie in the area of socio-emotional competences – with the guiding principle of "strategy follows people".

Strategic Competence No. 2 – A deep understanding of the principle theme "knowledge management is people business": The history of knowledge management in profit-making companies has all too often been marred by an exaggerated affinity to IT solutions. Because it is seen to be efficient (supposedly) it often lacks a thorough conceptual investigation of the processes.

In contrast, SOS Children's Villages has come to understand that the most appropriate and effective methods involve personal exchanges between people.

At SOS Children's Villages IT methods have always played a supporting role, rather than taking the lead part. The problem lies not with using IT systems to improve knowledge communication but rather in the fact that IT systems are often used aimlessly. Finally, the cost factor speaks highly in favour of using IT systems.

The nature of the core business of SOS Children's Villages makes it absolutely necessary for the organisation to put the experience and knowledge of the co-workers in the limelight. What is of particular importance are the "socio-emotional" competences such as building up reliable relationships (or working on relationships), the ability to empathise, the ability to take on responsibility for oneself and for others and the willingness to help. As an organisation, SOS Children's Villages actively attracts co-workers with these competences and helps them to develop further so that the organisation's vision can become a reality.

Thus, SOS Children's Villages already has a whole wealth of human resources and organisational competences. Many other companies and organisations still have to develop much of this. In his analysis of long-term economic cycles in 1996, Nefjodow emphasised the necessity of economists to deal more intensely with the aspect of psycho-sociological fitness as a source of growth and progress – having the ability to relate to values, having empathy and having the ability to relate to others are all high on the list.

The limits of transferability

Of course the recommendations and tips taken from the experiences made at SOS Children's Villages cannot be transferred on a one-to-one basis to a profit-making company, as there are at least two major differences to SOS Children's Villages:

First difference – The relevance of competition: First of all, we have to note that even for SOS Children's Villages, the battle to remain competitive has grown immensely over the past years. In some cases people are more reluctant to make donations, the number of competitors is rising, problems such as HIV/Aids are reaching pandemic proportions and conflicts between groups of people are increasing rather than diminishing. However, knowledge communication within the organisation faces far fewer challenges from inter-organisational rivalry than is commonly the case in most other (national and international) organisations. Securing copyrights to knowledge and experience totally contradicts the high ethical requirements that are the basis for the vision of SOS Children's Villages.

Second difference – Socio-emotional orientation: One of the most important differences between SOS Children's Villages and a profit-making company is the vital necessity of socio-emotional competences and behaviour within the organisation. This demands a high level of appreciation of values amongst its co-workers. This demand is almost diametrically opposed to the general practice in most other companies. Here emotions, empathy, honesty, authenticity and also co-operation are often negated and/or given a very low value. There are some fundamental, hugely problematic contradictions between profit making and caring for others. A case in point is the current wave of privatisation in Germany of health care services for the sick and elderly. Developments like this eradicate any form of considerate care and support on the part of the carer whose work is constantly undermined by the dictates of rigid time and cost cutting.

However, the differences mentioned above only limit the transferability of SOS Children's Villages' experiences to a certain extent. The high level of co-worker orientation as a basis of continuing success is exemplary and is also reflected in the Gallup polls (www.gallup.com) or the "Great Place to Work" awards (www.greatplacetowork.com).
The success of SOS Children's Villages is based on the guiding principle, "The human being as the heart of the matter". The edict, "The human being as a means," can no longer be seen as relevant today, not even in a world dominated by economics.

Literature

General Literature

Atteslander, Peter (2000): Methoden der empirischen Sozialforschung, Walter de Gruyter Verlag, Berlin und New York.

Habermas, Jürgen (2003): Erkenntnis und Interesse, Suhrkamp, Frankfurt am Main.

Harvard Business School (1998): Review on Knowledge Management, Harvard Business School Publishing, Boston.

IDEe-Häfele KEG (2005): Tipps und Tricks in: Die E-Learning Community, www.qualifizierung.com.

Lenzen, Dieter (Hrsg.) (2001): Pädagogische Grundbegriffe (Band 2). Jugend bis Zeugnis, Rowohlt Taschenbuch Verlag GmbH, Reinbek bei Hamburg.

Luhmann, Niklas (2002): Die Religion der Gesellschaft, Suhrkamp, Frankfurt.

Maleh, Carole (2001): Appreciative Inquiry. Bestehende Potenziale freilegen und für die Organisation nutzbar machen, in: Zeitschrift für Organisationsentwicklung, Heft 01/2001, Seite 32–41, Organisation- und Management-Entwicklung AG, Zürich.

Nefjodow, Leo A. (1996): Der sechste Kondratieff. Rhein-Sieg Verlag, St. Augustin.

Polanyi, Michael (1967): The Tacit Dimension, Doubleday Anchor, New York.

Probst, Gilbert/ Raub, Steffen/ Romhardt, Kai (2000): Managing Knowledge. Building Blocks for Success, John Wiley & Sons Ltd, Chichester.

Reinhardt, Rüdiger/ Eppler, Martin J. (Hrsg.) (2004): Wissenskommunikation in Organisationen. Methoden, Instrumente, Theorien, Springer-Verlag, Berlin.

Reinmann-Rothmeier, Gabi et al. (2001): Wissensmanagement lernen. Ein Leitfaden zur Gestaltung von Workshops und zum Selbstlernen, Beltz Verlag, Weinheim.

Schreiber, Horst/ Vyslozil, Wilfried (2003): Tracing our Roots, SOS-Kinderdorf International, Innsbruck.

Schmidt, Rolf (2003): Wissenskommunikation. Konzepte und Instrumente zur Verbesserung der gesellschaftlichen Nutzung von Wissen. Ergebnisse einer Literaturrecherche, in: Materialien Sozialer Ökonomie, www.isoe.de/literat/msoe21.htm.

UNAIDS, UNICEF and USAID (2002): A Joint Report on Orphan Estimates and Program Strategies, UNAIDS, UNICEF, USAID.

UNAIDS/UNICEF (2003): Children Orphaned by AIDS in sub-Saharan Africa, UN-AIDS/UNICEF Fact Sheet.

UNICEF – United Nations Children's Fund (2005): Millennium Development Goals learning module on Voices of Youth, What can you do to help end poverty? Fact Sheet, MDG1; http://www.unicef.org/voy/explore/mdg/explore_2203.html.

Verein Entdeckendes Lernen e.V. 2005: Projekt Tulpengarten, www.Tulpengarten.Entdeckendes-Lernen.de.

Wulf Christoph (2001): Einführung in die Anthropologie der Erziehung. Beltz Verlag, Weinheim.

SOS Children's Village Publications

Gigleitner, Carolina/ Rafetseder, Gerhild (2002): Harvesting – Report 2002, SOS Children's Village Hermann Gmeiner Academy, Innsbruck.

Hilweg, Werner/ Lechner-Kreidl, Christina (2002): Good Practice Workshops 2003/2004. In support of the SOS Children's Village Manual Implementation, SOS Children's Village Hermann Gmeiner Academy, Innsbruck.

Lechner-Kreidl, Christina (2003): Action Research. Good Practice Workshop Africa, 12–16 May 2003. Report by Action Researcher, SOS Children's Village Hermann Gmeiner Academy, Innsbruck.

Modungwa, Thembi (2002): Call for Good Practices Abstracts in Africa. Guidelines for Identification and Description of a Good Practice, SOS Children's Village Association South Africa, Johannesburg.

Modungwa, Thembi (2002): Continental Good Practice Workshop Africa. Action Plans, SOS Children's Village Association South Africa, Johannesburg.

Modungwa, Thembi (2003): Minutes of the Africa Good Practice Workshop, SOS Children's Village Association South Africa, Johannesburg.

Nguyen-Feichtner, Mai (2003): Action Research. Project Concept, SOS Children's Village Hermann Gmeiner Academy, Innsbruck.

Pittracher, Barbara/ Rudisch-Pfurtscheller, Andrea (2001): Project Description. Tracking Footprints – A study on the courses of the lives of former SOS children, SOS Children's Villages Hermann Gmeiner Academy, Innsbruck

Pittracher, Barbara/ Rudisch-Pfurtscheller, Andrea (2002): Tracking Footprints. Analysis of Questionnaire. Open Questions. Nr. 510/285 – Zimbabwe, SOS Children's Villages Hermann Gmeiner Academy, Innsbruck

Pittracher, Barbara/ Rudisch-Pfurtscheller, Andrea/ Westreicher, Bianca (2002): Tracking Footprints. Implementation Guide, SOS Children's Village Hermann Gmeiner Academy, Innsbruck.

Pittracher, Barbara/ Rudisch-Pfurtscheller, Andrea (2003): "When someone does research work ..." An international research project and its unexpected effects on SOS Children's Villages. (Paper presented at the Congress "Management of Educational Work: Evaluation and Organisational Development", Hamburg), SOS Children's Village Hermann Gmeiner Academy, Innsbruck

Pittracher, Barbara/ Rudisch-Pfurtscheller, Andrea/ Westreicher, Bianca (2004): Tracking Footprints. Global Report 2002/2003, SOS Children's Village Hermann Gmeiner Academy, Innsbruck.

Pittracher, Barbara/ Rudisch-Pfurtscheller, Andrea/ Westreicher, Bianca (2005): Tracking Footprints. Results and Recommendations. SOS Children's Village Hermann Gmeiner Academy, Innsbruck.

Rafetseder, Gerhild (2003): Harvesting – Report 2003, SOS Children's Village Hermann Gmeiner Academy, Innsbruck.

Rafetseder, Gerhild (2004): Harvesting – Report 2004, SOS Children's Village Hermann Gmeiner Academy, Innsbruck.

SOS-Kinderdorf International (2002): Human Resources Manual, Innsbruck.

SOS-Kinderdorf International (2002): Taking Action for Children. Strategic Plan 2003-2008, Innsbruck.

SOS-Kinderdorf International (2002): Who we are. Roots, Vision, Mission and Values, Innsbruck.

SOS-Kinderdorf International (2004): SOS Children's Village Manual, Innsbruck.

SOS-Kinderdorf International (2005): Family Strengthening Programmes Manual for the SOS Children's Village Organisation, Innsbruck.

Authors
Editors

Brandl, Astrid, Master's degree in Translation (English and French) in Innsbruck, London and Tours; Studies in General Management at the Management Center Innsbruck, major fields of study: Strategy and Human Resources Development; several years of experience as a qualified travel agent and licensed tourist guide; since 1997, a co-worker of SOS-Kinderdorf International; in 2003, nominated as director of the SOS mothers team of the SOS Children's Village Hermann Gmeiner Academy; since October 2004, assistant for organisational development in the office of the secretary-general; mother of the twins Christoph and Florian.

Hilweg, Werner, Dr., Doctor of Psychology (Vienna), psychotherapist, clinical psychologist; social quality assurance; director of the Hermann Gmeiner Academy quality assurance team; for many years, co-worker in the socio-educational department of the Austrian SOS Children's Village association; has organised numerous international knowledge communication projects.

Lechner-Kreidl, Christina, Master's degree in Educational Sciences; since 2001, co-worker in the quality assurance team of the SOS Children's Village Hermann Gmeiner Academy specialising in evaluation; previously, several years of educational work experience as head of a kindergarten.

Nguyen-Feichtner, Mai, Master's degree in Psychology; educational adviser to the SOS-Kinderdorf International Continental Office for Central & Eastern Europe, CIS/Baltic States in Vienna; currently, co-worker of the quality assurance team of the SOS Children's Village Hermann Gmeiner Academy specialising in development planning.

Reinhardt, Rüdiger, Prof. Dr, Organisational psychologist; Master's degree and PhD in Business Administration (management/economics); Head of the Department of Economics and Management at the Management Center Innsbruck; formerly, assistant professor at the Technical University of Chemnitz (Leadership and HRM) and professor at the University of St. Gallen (speciality: Knowledge Management); experience as a management consultant (strategy, HR, change management).

Rafetseder, Gerhild, Master's degree in Sociology; many years of experience in adult education and psycho-social work; until 2006 co-worker in the training team of the SOS Children's Villages Hermann Gmeiner Academy, speciality: human resources development, concepts for the profession of village directors and youth care staff members of SOS Children's Villages.

Rudisch-Pfurtscheller, Andrea, Master's degree in English/American and Roman Philology, qualified secondary school teacher for English and French; professional experience as a foreign language assistant in Toulouse, France; trained personality coach; since 1991, member of SOS Children's Villages staff; until 2006, co-worker of the SOS Children's Village Hermann Gmeiner Academy; speciality: research on childhood and youth in the international work field.

Salchegger, Karin, Master's degree in Religious Education and German Philology, qualified secondary school teacher; additional training as a print and broadcast journalist; professional experience as a teacher and broadcast journalist (Austrian television and radio); since 2002, co-worker of the public relations team of the SOS Children's Village Hermann Gmeiner Academy; specialities: editorial supervision of intranet and establishment of an internal specialist library;

Westreicher, Bianca, Master's degree in English/American and Roman Philology, speciality: literature; qualified secondary school teacher for English and Spanish; various study trips abroad (Spain, USA, Latin America); trained teacher for Integral Yoga; many years of work experience as a translator; currently, co-worker of the research team for childhood, youth and family of the SOS Children's Village Hermann Gmeiner Academy; speciality research on childhood and youth in the international work context.

Wilms, Stewart, Bachelor's degree in Economics, University of Calgary, Canada; assistant to the secretary-general of SOS-Kinderdorf International; director of various projects in the fields of strategy, organisational politics and organisational development; start of international career in Calgary, Montreal, with AISEC (a student organisation promoting the international transfer of management skills; vice-president of the international office in Brussels); since 1989, co-worker of SOS Children's Villages with various functions in the fields of management and organisational development in Eastern and Southern Africa as well as on an international level.

Picture credits

Cover photo: Dominic Sansoni
Photos of children's eyes: Marta Wenaas (Chap. 1), Sebastian Posingis (Chap. 2),
Katja Snozzi (Chap. 3/5), Alexander Gabriel (Chap. 4/6)
Other photos: Barbara Lill-Rastern (p. 100), Gerhild Rafetseder (p. 134, 136), Evelyn Winkler (p. 175, 177).

In 132 cou...

Croatia   Indonesia   Peru   N...
Lesotho   Lithuania
Niger   Rwanda   Taiwan   Togo
GreeceBelarus   Bangladesh
Kenya   Denmark
Cambodia   Finland   Turkey
Thailand   Czech Republic   Sri   Palestinian
Mozambio   Equatorial
Netherlands   Le
Malawi   Former Yugoslav Republic o...   Alg
Colombia   Cape   Burundi
French Polynesia   Chad   Belgium   Surinam
Democratic Republic of the   Côte d'Ivoire   Chi...
Nicaragua   Guinea   Honduras
Israel Burkina   Armenia   Costa
Dominican Neth...
Yugoslavia   Canada   Germany
Bulgaria   Italy
Bosnia and
Portugal   Hungary   Central African
Cameroon   Mali
Tanzania   South   Ghana
Mauritius   Chile   Norway   Albania   Argentina
Northern
Venezuela   IcelandLaos   South
Kosovo   Zimbabwe
United States   Uzbekistan   Mexico

The SOS Children's Village Facilities and Programmes*

SOS Children's Villages		458
SOS Youth Facilities		359
SOS Kindergartens		229
SOS Hermann Gmeiner Schools		180
SOS Vocational Training Centres		102
SOS Social Centres		415
SOS Medical Centres		56
SOS Emergency Relief Programmes		12
TOTAL		**1.811**

Number of countries and territories in which SOS Children's Villages is active	132
Number of children in SOS Children's Villages	49,469
Number of young people in SOS Youth Facilities	16,307
Number of children attending SOS Kindergartens	23,575
Children and young people attending SOS Hermann Gmeiner Schools	101,310
Beneficiaries of SOS Vocational Training Centres	15,243
Persons attending SOS Social Centres	254,149
Persons attending SOS Medical Centres	452,356
Persons supported through SOS Emergency Relief Programmes	390,781

*December 2006

Franz Huber

Social Networks and Knowledge Spillovers

Networked Knowledge Workers and Localised Knowledge Spillovers

Frankfurt am Main, Berlin, Bern, Bruxelles, New York, Oxford, Wien, 2007.
158 pp., num. tab. and graphs
ISBN 978-3-631-55631-3 · pb. € 34.–*

There has been much discussion about the importance of networks for regional economic development and knowledge dissemination. However, the inflationary use of the notion *networks* is often based on rather metaphorical, at worst fuzzy meanings. This book explores ways for more rigorous research on knowledge networks, critically discussing quantitative social network analysis. A theoretical framework for meaningful interpretations in quantitative network research is developed. Afterwards, the monograph links social network analysis to research on localised knowledge spillovers. Here the role of communities and networks of knowledge workers is investigated. The book illustrates how social network analysis can provide fruitful perspectives for further research on knowledge flows.

Contents: The position of social network analysis within the sociological research tradition · Localised knowledge spillovers: theoretical perspectives and critique · Communities and networks of knowledge workers, space and social network analysis · Perspectives of social network analysis for analysing localised knowledge spillovers

Frankfurt am Main · Berlin · Bern · Bruxelles · New York · Oxford · Wien
Distribution: Verlag Peter Lang AG
Moosstr. 1, CH-2542 Pieterlen
Telefax 0041 (0) 32 / 376 17 27

*The €-price includes German tax rate
Prices are subject to change without notice
Homepage http://www.peterlang.de

Peter Lang · Internationaler Verlag der Wissenschaften